Coordination in Soccer

A new road for successful coaching

——————— **Pawel Guziejko** ———————

iUniverse, Inc.
New York   Bloomington

Coordination in Soccer
A new road for successful coaching

Copyright © 2009 Pawel Guziejko

iUniverse books may be ordered through booksellers or by contacting:

*iUniverse
1663 Liberty Drive
Bloomington, IN 47403
www.iuniverse.com
1-800-Authors (1-800-288-4677)*

*ISBN: 978-1-4401-5328-0 (pbk)
ISBN: 978-1-4401-5327-3 (ebook)*

Printed in the United States of America

iUniverse rev. date:6/25/09

Contents

INTRODUCTION

Soccer is my passion. Today, it would be hard to imagine my life without this amazing branch of sports, the most popular game in the world. Everyone is interested in soccer. It is played everywhere. Stadiums holding a hundred thousand spectators prove too small when it comes to international confrontations and, for that matter, sometimes even for local teams.

In sports, there are neither patent to guarantee continual victory nor can there ever be. The occasional sensational defeats suffered by well-established teams at the hands of secondary division teams are one of the elements that distinguish this branch of sports from many others. Soccer is a communicative sport and the modern game has become great theatre. It is not only the players who prepare for the game, but the fans too. International matches have a dimension all their own. Like their idols on the pitch, fans don their national colors and lustily sing their national anthems during official opening ceremonies.

Soccer and all of modern-day sports involve not only fans, the spectacle and the emotions engendered, but also the athlete's complete physical and psychological commitment.

I refer, of course, to the training required, its structure and control. The athlete's training regimen constitutes an essential element in both the measurement of the effects of players' efforts and the insurance of a rational selection of means and methods for achieving particular and general skills.

One of the elements that make up general physical fitness, besides strength, agility, endurance and speed, is motor coordination. In this book I would like to draw attention to precisely this aspect and its teaching in the sports training of children and youngsters at different stages of their soccer and general physical development. This textbook is addressed first and foremost to soccer coaches and instructors working with children and youngsters, but also to professionals working in this field of sports, and those working in all institutions connected with soccer, sports and physical education generally.

The book consists of three parts. The first provides a definition of motor coordination. It examines the component parts of motor coordination and its essential effect in increasing the technical and tactical abilities and the effectiveness of a soccer player's game at all stages of training.

Part two contains a description of the exercises and soccer games for various age groups. The common feature of all these exercises is actual training with a ball, which should always be the basis of coaching the young. I have made every attempt to ensure that all the exercises presented and their various forms approximate the conditions in which the actual game is played.

The third part considers questions connected with one-on-one play and the effect of coordinative training on the development of this very important element of playing soccer.

Modern soccer places enormous requirements on the player, including coordinative skills. During a game, various kinds of action arise where coordinative motor abilities must be at their peak. I refer here to trotting, sprinting with and without the ball, sudden stops and turns, jumps, slide tackles, one-on-one duels etc. This is why I have tried to show readers that exercises that use actual elements of the game and also shape motor coordination abilities are the best means of achieving not only the highest level of sporting ability, but also all-round skills. For in every soccer player, versatility is the priceless element most in demand. A frequent change of position, a reduction in the traditional division of roles for players with typically offensive or defensive tasks, and close-quarter situations are all further proof of how important motor coordination is in all sports training, but particularly in soccer.

I hope everyone appreciates that work with youngsters is the most important task for every sports club. It must be remembered that our aim is to prepare players for the actual game of soccer, which is why soccer education should always be at the highest professional level. I hope that this textbook will encourage and help all those involved in training children and youngsters.

I would like to emphasize that the majority of the exercises to be found in this publication have been applied in my own work with youngsters at various stages of training. They may be used at one's own discretion, adapting them if necessary to the conditions in which one has to work.

I wish every success and job satisfaction to all those coaching soccer skills to the young.

I. THE THEORY OF SOCCER COORDINATION

1.1. The notion of motor coordination and coordinative motor abilities as formulated by various authors.

The underlying premise of this book is that motor coordination can and must be developed throughout an athlete's training. We understand this term to denote man's ability to carry out motor actions that are complex in terms of coordinative relations, the ability to transfer smoothly from one set of closely coordinated movements to others, and also the ability to rapidly execute new motor actions according to unexpected tasks as they arise (Bednarski 2000).

Motor coordination is a very complex physical property. It depends on many factors: sex, age, motor talents and skills (the main factor). It also depends on the efficiency of the motor apparatus or physique. In view of the variety of motor forms, we shall divide coordination into general and specific.

General coordination enables the rational execution of various motor actions, regardless of the sport being played. Every sportsman aiming at overall development should work on his coordination. In view of the fact that this development must outstrip sporting rivalry, general coordination should be developed as early as possible.

Specific coordination is the ability which makes it possible to accomplish various complex movements quickly, smoothly and precisely. Therefore coordination training is closely connected with an individual's motor talents, enabling each sportsman to increase the efficiency of his/her specific training. Coordination development is achieved by the repetitious execution of previously defined movements and elements of sport specific special techniques. From my own experience I can say that sportsmen with lower height parameters are able to learn more quickly to execute complex motor tasks and more rapidly transfer from one set of closely coordinated movements to others.

Coordinative abilities are conditioned by the state and level of development of the nervous system. They are defined as integrated psycho-physical properties that are predominantly dependent on the processes of steering and controlling movement, whose "limited basis is the central nervous system" (Raczek 1991).

The whole process of coordinative skill preparation should embrace the following abilities (Raczek 1986):

- **quick reaction**
- **balance**
- **sense of rhythm**
- **differentiation**
- **orientation**
- **adaptation and transfer**
- **feedback**

The above mentioned components of coordinative preparation are of the highest importance in soccer skills development. The level of motor coordination at every stage of soccer development strongly affects the quality and pace of acquiring new and better techniques. Soccer is one discipline in which coordination plays a very important role. A soccer player must adapt during the game to conditions that are changeable and difficult to predict. Improvement of a soccer player's coordinative abilities should place at every stage of training. The use of the exercises in this book, both with and without a ball, will provide the foundation for acquiring these skills.

Motor coordination is understood still differently by Rudolf Kapera and Dariusz Śledziewski (1997), who claim that it is also the ability to feel one's own movement (sensitivity of receptors, the so-called sensitivity to muscles and joints) and on this basis the skill of eliminating mistakes is founded. This means (obviously in its simplest terms) that the motor talented child is one who more quickly perceives the incorrect execution of a given exercise and is able to introduce corrections more effectively.

A child's weak level of development in coordinative motor abilities in soccer will be a brake on the achievement of a high level of mastery in the sport. Therefore an exact formation of exercises at all stages of development mandatory to correct and further develop technical and tactical development of the athlete's general efficiency. Determining accurately a young soccer player's current coordinative abilities provides the coach with a firm and rational basis for the athlete's development.

Zbigniew Witkowski and Wladimir Ljach (2004) provide other definitions of motor coordination, writing that it is one of the most important resources (in particular its component parts) for increasing the technical and tactical level of a soccer player's mastery of the game and his effectiveness at all stages of training. This means that to a greater or lesser degree all coordinative motor abilities participate in the execution of every motor action and, depending on the type of that action, some of those abilities are engaged more and others less.

It could therefore be said that coordination, as a process, embraces the adaptation of all the components of a given movement towards an optimum solution in a specific situation during the game. The physical expression of coordination thus understood is first and foremost precision and economy in the executed motor action. Modern soccer places very high requirements on the game's participants. Today's game may be described as one requiring dynamics and speed. Without suitable physical, technical, tactical and mental preparation, a player cannot today be successful in the highest levels of the game. Exceptionally important for the modern soccer player are coordinative motor abilities and the formation of the same by means of drills and other forms of training. Based on my past work as a coach and observation of players during matches, I can say that a sportsman poorly prepared in terms of coordination and technique has no chance of being selected for high-level adult soccer. I say this because the great majority of a soccer player's actions are oriented towards instant solutions of technical and tactical tasks under constantly changing conditions and situations during a game.

Recognition of technical and tactical conditions

in the field of play along with motor coordination provided by training affect the quality of a skilled response during play. In the modern game, the player must not only co-operate well with his team-mates but also simultaneously resist opponents' actions, react rapidly to every movement of the ball, respond to climatic changes and variability of pitch surface. He must also make accurate decisions within a limited space of the field while under the pressure of opponents and time. The modern soccer player should moreover possess the physical ability to rapidly change direction and speed, particularly when avoiding a tackle, not to mention sudden changes of direction when running with or without the ball. He must feint, run short distances and jump. Mastery to a very high degree in the above-mentioned elements affect a soccer player's abilities during the game and is inseparably connected with coordinative preparation and training, which especially in soccer should be understood to be three fold: technical, individual and team.

Coordinated action of skeletal muscles and the central nervous system is controlled and regulated by a sequence of processes occurring in the human organism that is defined as coordination (Schreiner 2007).

Coordination is therefore a complex notion pertaining to the learning, control and use of bodily movements in various forms.

Translating the above definition into the language of sport, we can say that in soccer training, we must develop complex reactions, based on motor coordination exercises. During such sessions, players can more rapidly assimilate technical elements and develop them economically and precisely. They will later more rapidly adapt these exercises to the unexpected situations they meet on the pitch.

1.2. A breakdown of coordinative motor abilities and their importance in modern soccer

Coordinative abilities matter enormously during the playing of a match. My observation of various stages of soccer training have permitted me to draw the conclusion that coaches dedicate too little time to coordinate development and worse still, some skip them entirely. Many coaches, instructors and soccer adepts will ask themselves: is this a mistake? After all, we develop other characteristics, such as speed, strength and endurance. We work on improving tactical elements and develop the technical elements that constitute or in soccer are closely connected with motor coordination. The question remains: are we shaping them sufficiently and how? Are we selecting suitable exercises for the formation of coordinative motor abilities? Are these applied exercises reflected in the actual soccer game?

To answer the above questions I shall use an example. If you follow soccer games attentively, you will soon notice that the game often takes place within a small space of usually a maximum 15 – 20 square feet and it progresses at a very rapid pace. In which case, what is the sense of technical coordination training using exercises that depart from or are fundamentally different from what takes place in a modern soccer game? More than once I have been a witness of training units, in which exercises, and games particularly, are held on large open spaces, without the pressure of opponents, without interplay against two or three contacts, without demanding any precision from younger age groups or precision and speed from more senior players. We need to realize that sportsmen who are educated by means of coordination and technical training separate from the actual game will stand little chance of being selected for high-level adult soccer. It is important to remember that the high-priority and long-range goals in work with children and youngsters is their preparation for the game at a high level, in terms of its technical, tactical, physical, and mental aspects. Unfortunately, practice shows that for many coaches, and sadder still, for parents, the most important priority is the final score and not how the young players are coached. This is negatively reflected in coordination and technical training, where the aim, i.e. the winning of the next match, means that the most important aspects of soccer education, and without a doubt motor coordination is one such aspect, are pushed into the background or not taken into consideration at all in the training process! The conclusion drawn is that the majority of sportsmen, trained in the way described above, executing motor actions with and without the ball on a reduced area of play and in addition, under pressure from opponents, will as a result be of a low level of coordination and they will not be in any position to win one-on-one tackling duels, speed by an opponent, pass with precision etc.

Therefore, to be able to freely and smoothly move with and without the ball and to execute various rapid and dynamic motor movements, every soccer player needs well thought out and developed motor coordination training that abounds in exercises shadowing and mimicking the actual situations arising in the play of the game.

In providing this breakdown and short description of coordinative motor abilities, my intention is for every reader to appreciate their importance for soccer. Further parts of this book will show in what areas soccer training is required and how it may be developed.

The ability to react quickly permits a player to undertake immediate and purposeful motor action at a defined signal. The skill level of this ability is measured by the time in which the motor action has been executed (for example passing the ball in tempo to a team-mate positioned in an open space).

Modern soccer requires from players rapid reactions in many difficult playing field situations. In actual conditions of competition, the player receives and processes an enormous amount of information. It is therefore the soccer player's immediate task to select the right signal in relation to the specific situation occurring, so that his actions are to the advantage of his team. Players having this ability to an advanced degree will be in a position to:

- **carry out actions with or without the ball at the right pace, i.e. adequate to the situation occurring on the field;**
- **choose the optimum technical and tactical solutions to surprise an opponent.**

It should not be forgotten that this ability of rapid reaction is also one of the basic elements of the game for the goalkeeper's position. In serious competition, the goalkeeper has to excel in many specific actions. Play in the penalty area depends very much on him: for example whether or not to come out of the penalty area or to center the ball, his own reaction to the ball's flight path etc. The majority of the opponent's attacks end with him and he begins the majority of his own team's offensive actions. In other words, he is able to rapidly begin a counter-attack or slow down his team's game. These specific elements are the object of the goalkeeper's speed of reaction which must be conditioned by his training. These abilities must be developed to the highest degree in those playing in this position.

During a match, we observe a whole range of changing pitch situations. So it must be remembered that during the planning of training units and at every stage and level of training, we must develop and shape the young player's ability to rapidly react to the complex situations taking place during an actual game. For instance, we must use drills that set up a one-on-one game, where the player having possession of the ball must not only avoid being tackled by the opponents but also exchange one-touch passes with one or two neutral players also participating in this exercise.

Equilibrium is the maintenance of good balance and correct body position or the immediate recovery of balance and position while executing motor actions. Equilibrium also appears in the balancing of a given object, for instance juggling a ball. It must be remembered that this skill must be developed to adequately meet the conditions arising in the game, and so we need to apply exercises based on:

o   change of direction with and without the ball;

o   one-on-one game (dribbling, body play);

o   kicking and trapping of the ball in complex forms (particularly from the air);

o   goalkeeping techniques (punching, diving for the ball with a fall to the ground).

All of the above examples confirm how important it is to balance and control the ball. Drills teaching and reinforcing these required motor actions ensure control of the ball.

The effects of the proper improvement and development of this ability are:

o   precise passing to team-mates;

o   well-aimed shooting at the goal.

The ability of _sensing rhythm_, i.e. a feeling for the rhythm of movement in soccer, is seen as a corollary of the player carrying out his own motor actions. In order to force an opponent to make a mistake, soccer players apply changes of rhythm, feinting and "faking out" by expert dribbling of the ball. In other words, a player adapts the rhythm of his running to his opponent or forces his own in order to achieve the aim he has set himself, for example, beating his opponent in a one-on-one game. In soccer this ability is mainly seen in:

○ a change of pace in running (deceleration, acceleration);

○ regulation of the pace of the game.

The ability of *differentiation* is defined as a "feel for time and pace". The basis of the ability of differentiation is the precise perception of strength, time and space during the execution of a motor action aimed at an optimum motor solution (Chmura 2004). Development of this ability should include exercises in "feel of the ball," for example intercepting and kicking the ball as it comes flying at various velocities, and the use of various parts of the body to do so.

The ability of *orientation* permits one to define the position of one's own body during motion in time and space. Modern soccer has very high requirements with regard to the accomplishment of this ability during play. Coaches expect from players the quickest possible positioning of themselves on the playing field in relation to team-mates and opponents, depending on the conditions and situations occurring during the game, and an absolute awareness of just where the ball is at a given moment. When teaching this ability, coaches must utilize small games, in which the main emphasis is on positioning, as in 2 against 1 or 3 against 2 drills in a limited area.

The ability of *adaptation and repositioning* is the skill of assessing the situation during a game and rapidly adjusting to a change in conditions. In other words, the player must try to foresee his opponent's or team-mate's passes (must be able to "read the game" well). We develop this ability by applying a broad program of technical as well as tactical exercises. But let's not forget that we should use particular technical elements depending on specific tactical requirements: for example winning a one-on-one duel with a pass to a neutral team-mate and moving to an open space on the field.

The ability of *feedback* is understood as the execution of a motor task when all movements of the body co-operate with one another and simultaneously are well coordinated. This is a question of good organization of those parts of the body which participate in movement. A team sport like soccer requires the execution of many complex coordinative motor actions. A player must combine individual elements in a chain of actions in order to correctly solve any tasks the game presents (for example a player heads the ball with a jump, falls, gets up moving without the ball, dribbles the ball, then loses possession again and finally takes back possession from his opponent with a slide tackle – all within a few seconds). It can be seen from this example that the player executes a sequence of complex coordinative movements, where a special ability is closely linked with general efficiency. These combined abilities are of the utmost importance during a game of soccer, where in order to achieve his aim, a player must unite individual movements into a coordinated series of complex motor actions (as a further example: in a game of one-on-one, on obtaining possession of the ball a forward must avoid being tackled by a defender, dribble the ball and take a shot at the goal). All of this must be undertaken within the confines of a specific space and time.

Today's soccer places all kinds of coordinative requirements on participants in the game. A player must know how to solve the tasks that the game generates from one second to another. The modern soccer player with well developed motor coordination should at one moment co-operate well with team-mates and also effectively oppose attacks by opponents. His reactions to the pitch, the weather conditions and the movement of the ball should be the right ones. Decisions taken on the playing field must be quick and accurate, particularly under of training conditions of continuous pressure from opponents. *That is why the planning* should take into account at its every stage the development of motor coordination and coordinative motor abilities. The well trained and developed young player entering the adult soccer world must also be prepared in terms of his coordination. At particular stages of training, from youngster to junior, players must receive regular portions of varied coordinative exercises. The coach must use all possible kinds of games and exercises involving those situations that occur in the game. It must be remembered that the achievement of a high level of sport in this discipline is not possible without improvement and development of motor coordination through thoughtful and responsible sports training.

1.3.   Development of coordinative motor abilities at particular stages of training.

According to Rudolf Kapera and Dariusz Śledziewski (1997), in the development of coordinative abilities it is possible to specify the optimum age for undertaking training, which is as follows:

o   for a feeling of balance – 9-14 years of age,

o   for a feeling of rhythm – 8-12 years of age,

o   for speed of reaction – 7-11 years of age,

o   for muscular feeling – 7-13 years of age,

o   for agility (as a comprehensive form of coordinative abilities) – 8-13 years of age.

A breakdown of the above clearly signals that development of coordination ensures the best results in the 7-14 age stages. It also shows at what age and in what period of training it is best to develop coordinative abilities. Viewed from the perspective of human physiology, the period between 7 and 14 sees a dynamic and universal development of the whole organism. During these years, the nervous and muscular systems develop particularly intensely. Both systems are closely linked with motor coordination. As Chmura (2004) correctly assurts, coordination is the mutual co-operation of muscles in the process of motion. It follows that when a higher level of coordination is reached, the expenditure of energy in the execution of any given movement will be less. This ensues from the fact that rigorous development of these systems provides excellent conditions for improving movements that are complex in terms of their degree of difficulty and for learning new motor actions.

We should develop coordinative motor abilities in the training process according to the following rules:

- learning new, varied and more complicated movements that feature all the conditions of serious competition through the use of a broad range of new and varied exercises corresponding to the soccer game at every level of training.

- perfecting learned exercises by conducting them under various space and time conditions.

Every training unit must be planned to provide methods and exercises which are designed to achieve the main objective of that specific unit. Our choice of objective depends on what we want to achieve and what we want to work on during training sessions in order to obtain these desired effects. It unfortunately often happens that coaches choose unsuitable methods to achieve the aims they have set and thus fail to achieve the intended results. In order to develop motor coordination correctly and to obtain satisfactory results throughout a training cycle, one should:

- make regular changes to the exercises conducted, for example: carry out the same exercise at a varied pace, in opposite directions and using other, more difficult opening positions.

- combine a single simple motor form with several other more complex ones (for example dribbling the ball between cones, passing the ball with an inside touch to a team-mate, jumping with both feet over a hurdle and heading a second ball thrown in by a partner)

- apply the exercise with a time limitation (for instance juggling the ball between cones within a set time or timing reaction speed exercises)

- frequent alteration of the physical conditions in which an exercise is conducted (for instance changing the width or length of the pitch, exercising with a partner, in threes etc, using balls of various size and weight, not necessarily soccer balls)

- the use of various signals (visual, acoustic)

- using exercises that bring other muscle groups into play; such exercises must follow one after another

- carrying out various motor actions symmetrically, which in practice means the skill of playing with both legs simultaneously.

In my own coaching work I try to plan each training unit precisely. Then, after sessions, I carefully analyze whether the original objective has been achieved. I proceed the same way in planning coordinative exercises, and since in soccer these are inseparably connected with the technique of executing a given motor task, I try to ensure the players practice those elements that are most often executed in actual game conditions. In other words, every exercise should be subordinated to situations which the soccer player must face during the game, as well as motor coordination exercises which are so essential an element in the development of every young soccer player (for example running between cones while simultaneously passing a tennis ball around the waist – one-touch passing of the ball to a partner using the inside of the foot – the execution of a slide tackle on the same ball after playing it). Obviously one should always choose exercises with regard to the skill level of the particular players playing in the team.

The player in today's soccer has many difficult and complex tasks to solve requiring him to combine motor actions. That is why in the development of motor coordination, we should teach those elements that are progressively more technically complex and of a greater degree of difficulty, particularly at the stage of training for those between 10 and 13 years old. At this age, players learn very quickly and assimilate new motor habits, including those that are more complex. The exercises chosen should contain elements of training that concentrate on coordination with and without the ball (as often as possible with the ball). These should be achieved by various other aides: hurdles, speed hoops, balls of various types and sizes, mattresses etc. The training exercises should be inseparably connected with soccer techniques. Motor coordination developed to a high level in conjunction with impeccable technique is what differentiates great soccer players from the average. Developing these two elements in a single athlete is the sole purpose of every coordination exercise.

In the introduction, I wrote that development of coordination gives the best results in the 7-14 age stages. I would like however to draw attention to the fact that training today begins as early as the age of 5 and sometimes even earlier. And so writing about motor coordination, I shall briefly characterize how it should develop beginning at even earlier stages of training.

I would divide early training at the age of 5 to 10 into two parts. The first of these concerns younger school age children between 5 and 7 years of age. The second concerns the preparation stage for those between 7 and 10 years of age.

The best method to develop motor coordination in the younger group is to use creative games involving various themes and movements. We must remember to ensure exercises are suitable to the age group in question, their needs, capabilities and exercising skills. A child at this stage of development is not able to concentrate his attention on one specific element or exercise for any length of time. Application of the same, continually repeated games at this particular training stage will cause the child to become bored with such sessions, and as a result, he/she may lose interest in soccer. The common aim of coaches working with this age group should therefore be to use fun games involving varied movements that simultaneously provide basic and simplified forms of coordinative motor exercise. The development of all coordination should proceed from the simplest to the more complex, from the easier to the more difficult. A basic element should also be a positive attitude shown by the coach and a smile on the child's face from the pleasure and joy at having successfully executed these motor tasks.

Exercises should contain elements of jumping, various forms of running, turning on the spot, changes in the direction of motion and mimicry (for example imitation of animal movements), while remembering about simple exercises with the ball!

Various forms of rivalry are also a good thing to include in any planning of training units. Let's remember to ensure sessions don't become too schematic or lead to monotony. I mean not only the multiple repetition of the same game, but also the execution of motor actions that are identical in terms of their sequence. For example, many coaches apply running games, often without the use of a ball, where one person must catch the others. The basis of this game involves children moving forward, sometimes changing just the direction in which they are running. Here, the development of motor coordination takes place with regard to just a single aspect, namely the changing of direction, but in fact should be achieved in many elements. So every exercise must develop several basic elements (for example, the coach may initiate the same game so that the player practicing dribbles a ball within a limited area in which hoops are laid out.) To avoid being caught, the player must get the ball in the circle made by the hoop and then tap the ball twice with the sole of his foot. Then he must find another ball and roll the ball twice with the sole of his foot). In the example above, the means applied are simple, but we achieve the coordinative effects in a considerably shorter time and with the advantage of developing techniques and coordination desired in the later stages of training.

Exercises must be suitably adapted to the child's psychological state. The child must draw pleasure from the proposed motor tasks. An effective game in conjunction with the achievement of simple coordinative motor tasks will be the basis for learning more complex movements at later stages of training.

The stage of *initial preparation* (7-10 year-olds) is the key period in their developmental age when children should be taught and should develop the majority of coordinative motor abilities. The most important of these in soccer, indispensable for carrying out motor actions, include: differentiation, orientation, adaptation, speed of reaction and feedback of movements. It is precisely the development of these elements that should constitute one of the aims of planning each and every training unit. Neglecting the development of one of these will make it impossible to master the sport which must be the goal of every coach working with children and youngsters.

Motor coordination is closely linked with the appropriate development of motor skills (in soccer, this means technical skills). One of its aims is to instill the good habit of accomplishing a given motor task (for example inside-outside dribbling). So at this stage of training, coordinative elements must be included until the player has assimilated the correct habit of accomplishing a given motor action. Because the combining of these two elements (coordination and technique) permits the player to avoid motor actions becoming totally automatic (for example if a player's motor task is inside-outside dribbling between cones and he repeats this exercise at each training session, this leads to automation of the movement, and as a consequence to just the simple execution of this exercise, which has little in common with the actual game. But if execution of this same exercise will be one of the several tasks in a motor related game, where one should also carry out changes of direction while running backwards and forwards without a ball, then this exercise will lead to the desired effects in the development of coordinative motor abilities in combination with soccer technique, and so will be effective in preventing stereotype techniques from setting in.

This stage of training should be characterized by the application of games that are more difficult in terms of the motor skills involved, particularly in the initial phase of the training unit and so during the warming up. In these exercises, one should often move from individual elements to more complex motor elements, not forgetting about the need for these to co-operate with technical elements. Exercises should often take place in conditions that vary with regard to space and time, for example passing the ball back and forth to a partner using the inside part of the foot on a limited field, so that the player may better adapt to the conditions met in an actual game. One should not forget about exercises forcing players to make rapid decisions and to quickly react, this being one of the more important elements in modern soccer. For example, in a departure from a simple motor task such as the tossing of a tennis ball, one may add the execution of two claps of the hands and catching of the ball before it falls to the ground and then the execution of a complex motor task, for example passing the soccer ball using the inside of the foot in conjunction with the passing of a tennis ball using one's hands, this carried out simultaneously and with a partner.

Our work at this stage should be to develop a skilled level of coordinative abilities and this skill level will determine how well new more and more complex motor actions can be added.

The basic learning stage (10-13 year-olds) involves perfecting the already taught motor actions and simultaneously learning difficult, complex forms of movement. To perfect here means to apply a repetitive method of executing motor tasks, applying various and varied exercises, in which the aim is uniform and unvarying. Again an inseparable element in each training unit should be the skilful mixing and combining of coordinative with technical exercises. The main goal, as always, of such exercises must be development of coordinative motor abilities in conjunction with technique in conditions of serious competition.

Players in this age group very quickly assimilate new, often unusually difficult motor habits. Remembering this, one should use exercises with balls of various sizes and weights. One should regularly make use of the exercises in which the player must use two soccer balls, (for example dribbling two soccer balls simultaneously). The training exercises should be carried out individually as well as with a partner or groups of 3 or 4, which additionally increases players' motivation to improve their skills and permits them to concentrate on a given motor task.

The stage between 14 and 16 years of age is the time to improve both simple and complex motor forms. Exercises carried out with and without a ball should be continued. Improvement in coordinative elements should be drilled and these exercises should reflect situations that the soccer player faces during an actual game (for example, player A executes a summersault, then passes the ball to player B, who one-touch passes it back to A and this is followed by a one-on-one game).

One of the most important goals at this stage is the skill of maintaining earlier developed coordinative motor abilities at the same or a higher level. This makes it possible to increase the technical and tactical qualifications of the players we train. More than once at this stage of training I have come across players whose motor coordination was at a very low level. The result of this was poor reactions to complex technical and tactical elements. To repeat, nobody has previously managed to suitably develop coordinative motor abilities and then combine them with technical exercises. We tend to forget that motor coordination to a large degree aids applied technical skills in the resolution of the tasks met in the soccer game.

Whereas in previous stages of training it was mainly

precision of the exercises carried out that mattered, now, while maintaining precision, one should without delay increase the speed at which motor actions are carried out.

In today's soccer the pace of the game is very rapid. The players of particular formations must react immediately to defensive and offensive actions. The too slow execution of a motor task may have dramatic results and so may end with the loss of the ball, a foul and in the worst case, the loss of a goal. That is why during training sessions it is important that we coaches rapidly and dynamically carry out those particular exercises that combine elements of coordination and technique.

We cannot forget about improving coordinative and technical elements when applying exercises for particular formations. For the forward: running between cones without the ball, then dribbling the balls as quickly as possible over a 15 foot section, then passing to a partner who with a one-touch passes it back and on receipt of the ball, the playing of a one-on-one game. In this case, the proposed exercises should take into account positions on the playing field and situations arising in the game that are faced by a given formation. For the back (defender): jumping over a hurdle - the execution of a slide tackle on a standing ball – returning backwards to a training marker – fighting with an adversary for possession of a ball passed by a partner. These exercises should be continually modified and carried out in changing conditions of time and space.

At the coaching stage (16-18 year-olds) the athlete

should have achieved the basics of soccer related coordinative motor abilities. If we presume that we are getting a group of players that have been properly led and excellently trained, then one should carry out the means of improving their coordination very quickly, in conditions made more and more difficult by the observant coach. These means should be varied. The higher the level of a player's training, the more difficult should be the forms of motor tasks we ask of him/her, never forgetting the basic motor tasks that the player must carry out during a game.

Summarizing this chapter, I list below the most important aspects of developing coordinative motor abilities at particular stages of training:

1. The applied exercises should be varied and unceasingly altered.

2. The selection of the exercises, their quantity and duration should mainly depend on the age and capabilities of the trained players.

3. The motor tasks carried out during exercises should take into account the nature and specifics of the soccer game.

4. Exercises carried out should take into account the following in this order:
   a) The precision of executing a motor action
   b) The speed of accomplishing a motor action while maintaining precision

5. The applied exercises should be carried out often but for short periods of time.

6. Exercises of a coordinative nature should be carried out during the warming up period, but must also fulfill the goals of the training unit.

7. Development of coordinative abilities should be combined with technical elements because these make possible the adaptation of the taught technical skills to the ever changing situations in the game.

8. We should develop motor coordination and its abilities at all stages of training.

II. EXAMPLE EXERCISES FOR MOTOR CORDINATION DEVELOPMENT IN SOCCER AT VARIOUS STAGES OF TRAINING

2.1. Younger School children (5-7 year-olds)

○ The players are divided into 4 teams of five. Two teams play against each other on two reduced playing fields measuring 45 x 30 feet. Each of the players on one team is given a (size 3) ball. Their task is to pass the ball from the right hand to the left or vice versa while running and to outrun the players of the opposite team whose task is to touch the player with the ball. The moment this touch happens, the touched player stands on one leg passing the ball from hand to hand, waiting until a partner frees him. He is freed by passing the ball to a team mate any way he chooses. The game may be played for an unlimited length of time.

○ Select 4 players from the team, who are to be called "tags". The remaining players receive a tennis ball. Their task is to pass the ball around the waist while running. The task of the tags is to catch players with balls. When a "tag" catches an opponent, the player caught stands with his legs astride and passes the ball around his waist. "Tagged" players are released from this position by a partner crawling on all fours between the caught player's legs. The game takes place on a playing field measuring 60 x 45 feet laid out with 4 markers. The game may be played for an unlimited length of time.

○ The players (each with a ball) dribble the ball in any direction on a playing field laid out by 4 markers. One- and-a-half-foot wide hoops are laid out in any position on the playing field. This game is called "colors". The coach has three sashes – red, green and yellow. The practicing player dribbles the ball in any direction and using any technique he chooses. At the moment the coach raises the red sash, players have the task of stopping the ball using the sole of the foot and changing the direction of their dribbling, also using the sole of the foot. When the green sash is raised, players must dribble the ball around any one of the hoops on the playing field clockwise and then anticlockwise. The yellow sash means they must touch the ball twice using the right and left foot with the simultaneous quickest possible dribbling of the ball.

○ We place a minimum 7 balls at random on a playing field 60 x 30 feet. We choose two players, whose task is to tag the remaining participants of the game. When a participant is caught, he stands and waits until any of his escaping partners can free him. The "tagged" players are released from their position by a team-mate on the playing field passing any of the 7 balls to them using the inside of the foot. On receipt of the ball, the caught player must trap it with the sole of a foot and can then rejoin the game running away from the two "catchers".

o "Tag pairs", in which players practice in pairs. The coach chooses two pairs, which will be the proverbial "tag". On a field marked out by means of 4 training flag staffs we lay 8 balls of various sizes at random. The pairs of players hold hands and try to avoid being caught by the pair which is "tag". While moving around, the players may not split up. The moment this happens they swap over with the pair that was previously the "taggers". If any of the evading pairs find themselves by the ball and pass it using the inside of the foot, that pair is safe and cannot to be caught by the "taggers". No more than 5 passes may be carried out between the players in a pair.

o The team is divided into two groups of equal number. These teams stand opposite each other at a distance of three feet. Some 15 to 21 feet behind both teams we mark out a finishing line by means of a training marker. We give the teams conventional names, for example north and south. Each of the players of both teams is given a ball. At the password "north" the team so called runs back to its appointed finishing line, while the opposing team tries to catch one or more players before they reach the finishing line. The moment they manage to do so they win a point. Before the password "north or south" is called out, the players of both teams have the task of executing the following: a) inside touches the ball while simultaneously clapping their hands; b) running around the ball backwards and forwards, each time stop-touching it with the soles of their feet; c) dribbling the ball with the right foot changing place with their partner from the opposing team, then dribbling the ball back using the left foot.

- ○ Each of the players is given a ball and plays on a pitch indicated by means of 4 markers and measuring 60 x 45 feet. Individual training markers are set out at random. At a signal sounded by the coach, the players carry out the following tasks:

  - • dribbling the ball using the sole of the right foot to one such marker and on to the next marker using the left foot,

  - • passing the ball using the inside of the foot with a simultaneous sprint for the ball and the execution of a sit on the ball,

  - • passing the ball using the inside of the foot, then at a signal stopping the ball with the sole of the foot and turning round first to the right, then to the left,

  - • Moving backwards with a simultaneous passing of the ball by hands around the waist clockwise and anticlockwise,

  - • free inside-outside dribbling of the ball using the right and left foot in turn - at a signal sounded by the coach a quick move forward without the ball with a change in direction in front of the training marker and after the change in direction, running backwards.

○ This game is called "mimicking animals". The coach calls out the name of an animal and the practicing player must copy its movements with the ball, for example:

- "kangaroo" – at the word "kangaroo", The players dribble the ball using any technique they may choose and in any direction, then stop the ball using the sole of the foot and jump with both feet without the ball,

- "bear" – at this password players crawl on all fours after previously dribbling the ball and stopping it with the sole of the foot,

- "tiger" – The players carry out quick dribbling of the ball with frequent changes of the direction in which it is dribbled,

- "eagle" – players dribble the ball and simultaneously raise and lower their arms.

○ This game is called "shadow". Players have the task of copying the coach's movements with and without the ball. We can use the following exercises in this game:

- dribbling of the ball using the right foot and then stopping it with the sole of the left foot,

- dribbling of the ball and stopping the ball using the knee and running around the ball clockwise or anticlockwise,

- moving backwards while bouncing the ball with both hands,

- hopping on one leg around the ball clockwise, touching the ball twice with the soles of the feet and then hopping on the other leg around the ball anticlockwise,

- side step: every 3 steps, dribbling the ball around one's own axis counterclockwise and then clockwise,

- Inside touches while moving forward. Stopping the ball using the sole of the foot and execution of various positions, for instance lying on one's stomach or on one's back, a straight sit and a straddle.

o The "racecourse" game. We divide players into 4 teams of not more than 5. Each team must cover the racecourse (points are given for precision of execution in the first order, and only secondly for speed). The winning team is the first to be awarded 10 points. The racecourse for each team is illustrated in diagram 1.

Diagram 1

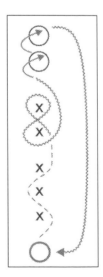

a) running forward with the ball in one's hands between a slalom of 4 training markers

b) inside-outside dribbling of the ball in a figure "eight" between two training markers,

c) dribbling the ball using the inside of the foot around a training marker clockwise and anticlockwise,

d) jumping in and out of 3 speed hoops arranged side by side,

e) dribbling of the ball using any technique the player may choose.

○ The "change position" game. We divide the team into two teams with the same number of players (not more than 6). The teams line up opposite each other six feet apart. We attribute a number from 1 to 6 to every player from each team. This game involves calling out the numerical passwords, so that on "one" being called, those players having this number must change places, moving in a way previously defined by the coach, for example forwards, backwards, forwards while simultaneously clapping hands, jumping with both feet etc. So that the game fulfils its purpose and is more intense, the coach is required to call out a larger quantity of numbers, for example 2 and 3 or 5, 3 and 1 etc. Players change places dribbling the ball with the technique asked of them by the coach.

○ All players are provided with balls (it is best to use a size 1 ball) and dribble on a playing field indicated by means of 4 markers. Each player is to position himself with the ball at one of the training markers and execute the following exercises:

- dribbling the ball in front of the marker one time using the sole of the right foot and stopping the ball using the sole of the left foot and then vice versa,

- moving clockwise around the marker without the ball and then inside-outside dribbling of the ball in the opposite direction,

- inside-outside dribbling of the ball one time using the right foot and stopping the ball using the sole of the same foot and then executing the same exercise using the left foot.

o The "stealing the marker" game – we mark out a playing area 45 feet long. Then we divide it into 3 equal zones each 15 feet long. In the middle zone we place about 15 markers at random and choose two players, who have the task of preventing the remaining players from collecting the markers. The rest of the players wait in zone 1 with the balls and at a given whistled signal, moving without a ball, must get across to zone 3, trying at the same time to steal a marker from the middle zone. When any of the remaining participants are touched by one of the two players from the middle zone, such a player must carry out a specified exercise with a ball in zone 1 or without a ball in zone 3. The following are examples of such exercises:

a) With a ball:
  - inside-outside dribbling of the ball around one's own axis and then turning on one's own axis without the ball,

  - passing the ball using the inside of the foot and trying to stop the ball with the knee the moment the ball is in motion,

  - dribbling the ball using the sole, stopping the ball with the foot and then moving backwards around the ball,

b) Without the ball:
- jumping with both feet twice, then hopping twice on the right foot and twice on the left foot and then twice again with both feet, then proceeding once with both feet and once on one foot,

- running while simultaneously clapping hands, then at a given signal changing direction, running backwards while clapping one's hands above one's head.

Please note: this exercise should be carried out before the players attempt to change zones and steal a marker.

o On half a playing field marked out by 4 flag staffs we set up slaloms of 4 markers each (there should be a minimum of 8 such slaloms). Moreover we arrange 4 markers set out diagonally, each some 9 feet apart (there should be a minimum of 5 of this type of slalom). Each of the players is given a (size 3) ball and a tennis ball held in the hand. At a given whistled signal, the players dribble the ball and simultaneously throw their tennis ball up in the air and catch it without letting it fall to the ground. At a double whistled signal, the players side step between the diagonally placed markers, simultaneously throwing their tennis ball up in the air again without letting it fall to the ground. At the password "dribble", players dribble the ball using any technique they may choose between the slalom markers. See diagram 2.

Diagram 2

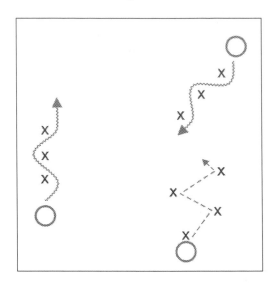

○ Each of the players is given two soccer balls. Each player is assigned one marker, next to which these two balls are arranged at a distance of three feet, one on each side. At a given whistled signal, all players carry out the following tasks:

- running forwards in any direction and at a given signal sit immediately on the ball,

- running backwards and at a given signal touching one ball twice with the sole of the foot and sitting on the second ball,

- hopping from one foot to another and at a whistle, running slalom between the balls and the marker and sitting on any ball,

- touching the first ball twice with the sole of the foot, running a slalom between the balls and the marker, inside touches the second ball, and running a slalom without the ball – diagram 3.

Diagram 3

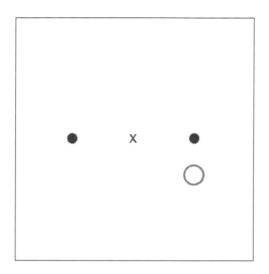

o   On a playing field measuring 15 x 115 feet we set up 10 training markers at random. Players are divided into pairs, which compete one-on-one on the playing field. The player nearest the ball receives a point for hitting as many markers as he can, which must take place as a result of dribbling the ball. The moment the ball is lost to his opponent, the first player becomes the defender and tries to prevent the new forward from hitting the markers.

o   This training exercise takes place in pairs and involves a one-on-one game. Every pair is assigned 4 markers set out 3 feet apart in a semicircle. The task of the player with the ball is to win the one-on-one duel and hit one of the markers which his opponent is protecting. Markers can be hit from one side only – diagram 4.

Diagram 4

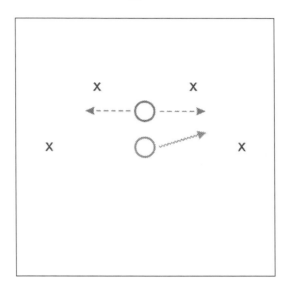

- ○ In the center of a playing field measuring 21 by 21 feet we set up a goal with a width of 5 feet. The game is played one-on-one. The player with the ball has the task of tackling his opponent and scoring as many points as possible by dribbling the ball through the goal which he can attack from either side. The moment the ball is lost, there follows an exchange of roles.

- ○ Players are selected in threes. Using markers we create two goals, each six feet wide and set up on the same line. The distance between goals amounts to 18 feet. Player A is given the position of defender and is positioned in the center between the goals. Players B and C take up positions opposite the goals. The exercise is begun by player B, who has possession of the ball. He tries to dribble the ball through one of the two goals and to pass to his partner on the other side or pass the ball using the inside of the foot through one of the goals without being tackled by the defender and losing the ball. Players receive one point for every successful attempt. There follows an exchange of roles the moment the defender successfully tackles the player – diagram 5.

Diagram 5

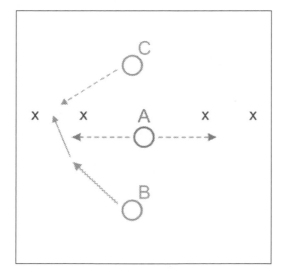

Pawel Guziejko

2.2. The initial preparation stage (7-10 years old)

○ Each practicing player is given a marker and keeps it in his left or right hand. Moreover, each player is in possession of a (size 3 or 4) ball. The players on half the field carry out inside-outside dribbling of the ball while simultaneously transferring the training marker from the right hand to the left or vice versa.

○ The players carry out inside-outside dribbling of the ball on half the field using the left foot, holding the training marker in the right hand. At a given signal, they change the foot doing the dribbling with a simultaneous transfer of the marker to the other hand, and so: right foot - left hand and vice versa.

○ The players (each in possession of two balls) carry out dribbling of these two balls simultaneously on half the field. At a given signal, they dribble one ball around the second ball using the outside of the foot. At the next signal, the same motor actions are carried out using just the inside of the foot.

○ A dozen or so tennis and soccer balls are arranged at random on a marked out area of playing field (the number of balls depends on the number of players). Players carry out the following actions:

- side step from ball to ball and at a given signal, inside touches a ball (the player inside touches the ball nearest to which he is positioned at a given moment);

- move backwards and forwards (the change in the direction occurs the moment the player finds himself next to any ball) and, at a given signal, dribble a tennis ball in any direction;

- run forward and execute a sit on the ball, then inside touches on any ball a minimum of 5 times followed by a straddle moving backwards and forwards with inside touches of the ball.

- hop from one foot to the other and, at a given signal, inside-outside dribbling of the ball (carried out without interruption) using the inside part of the right and then the left foot and then the outside of the right foot and vice versa (inside - inside - outside). Dribble a soccer and tennis ball in turn.

o On half the field, players (each with two soccer balls) carry out inside-outside dribbling of the ball using the right foot followed by the left foot in turn simultaneously passing the second ball around the waist. At a given signal, they change direction and the ball is passed around the waist from right to left or vice versa simultaneously changing the direction of the dribbling.

o The players position themselves on one half of the sports field (each being given two soccer balls). The players dribble one ball with inside touches in any direction. At a given signal, they jump up and catch a second ball while continuing to dribble the first ball by inside touches.

o The players are divided into two groups. Each group chooses one field marked by 4 training markers.

The players of both teams carry out dribbling of the ball:

- Forwards, using the sole of the foot and at a given signal, turning on their own axis;

- running backwards and at a given signal, dribbling of the ball around their own axis using the inside of the foot;

- inside-outside dribbling of the ball and at a given signal, executing a single scissors with a trapping of the ball using the sole of the foot and a simultaneous change in direction without the ball;

- dribbling of the ball using laces and at a given signal, the quickest possible run without the ball to the marked out field of the opposing team;

- players roll the ball in one spot using the sole of the right foot and stopping the ball using the sole of the left foot and vice versa. At a given signal, dribble the ball with a change in direction using the outside of the foot.

○ On a playing field we mark out a rectangle (90x60 feet), in the centre of which we mark out at random 4 small fields 15 feet in diameter indicated by means of four training markers. In two of these we arrange 10 training markers at random. Players carry out the following tasks:

- free dribbling of the ball on the whole of the marked out area using any technique they may choose;

- rapid dribbling of the ball in two of the 4 marked out fields using only the right foot;

- moving without the ball between the markers set up in the next two fields;

- dribbling the ball over the whole area using only the left foot;

- dribbling the ball using the laces twice with the right and twice with the left foot in two of the 4 marked out fields.

○ The players practice in pairs, each pair being given one ball and lining up next to one of the training markers. Player A stands with his back to player B. The distance between the players is 5 feet. Player A executes a "jumping jack" exercise, while player B dribbles the ball around the marker using the outside of the foot. At a given signal, A stands with his legs astride, while B passes the ball using the inside of the foot between the legs of A, who in the shortest possible time must try to take possession of the ball and stop it using the sole of his foot and pass it back to player B, who runs out to an open space on the field. After this is repeated several times, they exchange roles.

○ The players practice in pairs. Player A dribbles the ball one time using the sole of the right foot and once with the inside of the left foot and vice versa between two markers set at a distance of 9-12 feet apart. Player B stands behind a training marker with a tennis ball in his hands. At a given signal, player B throws the tennis ball to A, who must return it to player B as quickly as possible and continuing to dribble the ball using the above-mentioned technique.

○ The players practice in pairs. Player A executes a running slalom without the ball between four markers set at a distance of 3 feet apart. Player B stands with a ball next to a training marker set at a distance of 9 feet from the markers forming the slalom. After running slalom, player A one-touch passes the ball back using the inside of the foot to player B. While player A is running the slalom, player B touches the ball using the soles of the feet and passes it using the inside of the foot to player A at the moment player A finishes running the slalom.

○ The players practice in pairs. Player A stands with his back to player B. Both players are given balls. Players A and B carry out a double scissors over the ball until a signal is blown on a whistle, at which point the players exchange balls using the inside of the foot. After they exchange balls, the exercise begins again using the same technique.

○ On a whole playing field we use training markers to create exercise fields measuring 6x6 feet. The number of fields must correspond to the number of players. On each field we lay a speed hoop. Each player is positioned with a ball in one of 6 x 6 foot areas and individually executes the following exercises:

  • diagonal dribbling of the ball using the right foot, with a change in direction using the sole of the foot, then two jumps with both feet from the outside to the inside of the hoop;

- inside-outside dribbling of the ball using the inside part of the right and left foot then the outside of the right foot without interruption and vice versa with a change in direction using the outside of the foot. After dribbling, 4 jumps from one foot to the other from the outside to the inside of the hoop;

- dribbling of the ball with inside touches diagonally across the field, with single scissors in front of the marker. After dribbling, 4 jumps with both feet from the outside to the inside of the hoop;

- dribbling of the ball inside the foot with a "step over" change in direction, sprinting to the hoop and quickly running around it (clockwise, then anticlockwise) – diagram 6.

Diagram 6

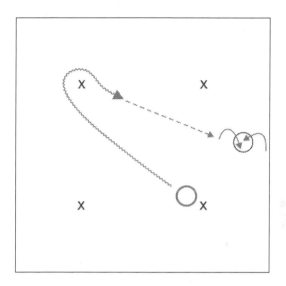

- The players practice in pairs. Both players are given balls. Players A and B dribble their balls opposite each other. When 3 feet apart, they exchange balls with a side pass using the inside of the foot and run for the ball passed by their partner. Then they trap the ball with the sole of their foot and changing direction, run back towards their partner.

- The players are divided into groups of six. Each group is assigned a circle made of 6 training markers. In the center of each circle we place a training marker (each must be of a different color). A player from each group positions himself next to one of the training markers forming the circle. Players carry out the following actions (all at the same time):

- dribbling of the ball using the right foot to the middle marker with a change in direction using the sole, then return dribbling of the ball using the left foot;

- the execution of a single scissors with a simultaneous dribbling of the ball to the middle marker, then return dribbling of the ball using the sole of the foot with a lap round the outer marker;

- dribbling the ball forwards to the middle marker using the sole of the foot. Then return dribbling the ball backwards using the sole of the foot and then exchanging the ball with the closest partner using the inside of the foot.

○ The players practice in pairs, one ball to a pair. Each pair is assigned 4 markers: 3 smaller ones in different colors and one larger, which is the same for each pair. Player A stands with the ball next to the larger marker. Player B stands opposite player A between the larger marker and the three smaller ones which are set out at a distance of six feet behind his back. At the coach's command, for example "yellow", player B turns round, touches that color marker and using the inside of the foot one-touch passes the ball back to player A. Before passing, player A touches the ball using the left and right soles of the feet in turn – diagram 7.

Diagram 7

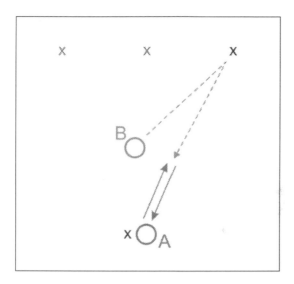

○ The players practice on a (45x45 foot) playing field marked out by means of 4 flag staffs and carry out the following exercises:

- dribbling of the ball using the inside of the right and left foot and the outside of the right foot carried out without interruption and then vice versa. At a signal, lying down on one's stomach, getting up immediately to continue dribbling using the above-mentioned technique;

- dribbling of the ball using the inside of the left foot and the sole of the right foot. At a given signal, exchange balls with any partner continue dribbling using the same technique;

- dribbling the ball twice using the laces of the right foot and twice using the laces of the left foot, then touching the ball 4 times using the sole. At a given signal, exchanging the ball with any partner using the outside of the foot after dribbling with it.

○ The players practice in pairs (every player with a ball). Players A and B progress in the same direction, each dribbling their ball. The distance between the players of one pair may not be greater than three feet. The players of each pair have the task of changing the direction of their dribbling and the pace of the action, with player A determining the technique of the change in direction of the dribble and the pace of the action. Player B's task is all the time to move as far as possible in line with player A (players must carry out all motor actions at the same time).

Variation: This exercise may be carried out without the ball while maintaining the same motor actions, and so changes in direction and the pace at which they run.

○ The players practice in pairs. Each pair is assigned one ball and three training markers arranged in the form of a triangle. Each player from a pair chooses one marker forming the triangle and positions himself next to it. Player A inside-outside dribbles the ball. Player B progresses without a ball opposite player A. Then player A passes the ball to player B, then progresses backwards to a free marker without the ball. Then player B passes the ball to player A, then progresses backwards without the ball to a free marker. See diagram 8.

Diagram 8

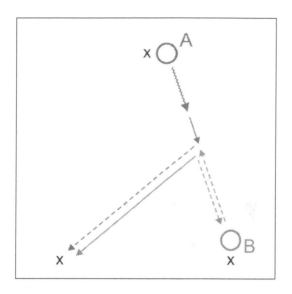

o The players practice in pairs. Each pair is assigned three training markers arranged in the form of a triangle and one ball. Player A chooses a marker forming the triangle and positions himself next to it. Player B places himself in the center of the triangle with the ball and dribbles it in any direction. Player A side steps, touching two of the three markers forming the triangle with his hand. After he touches a marker, using the inside of the foot he one-touch passes the ball back played by player B and progresses to the next marker where after touching it he again, using the inside of the foot, one-touch passes the ball back to player B. The roles are changed after 10 repetitions.

○ The players practice in pairs. Each pair is assigned three training markers, arranged in the form of a triangle, and one ball. Player A positions himself with the ball in the center of the triangle. Player B chooses a marker forming the triangle and places himself next to it. Player A passes the ball using the inside of the foot to player B and runs forward to a free marker. After trapping the ball, player B dribbles the ball, changing direction by using the sole of the foot in front of one of the two markers forming the triangle and passes with an inside touch to player A. The players change places after several repetitions.

○ The players practice in pairs. Each pair is assigned three training markers arranged in the form of a triangle and one ball. Players A and B each place themselves next to any marker forming the triangle. Player A is given the ball. Player B is without a ball. Players A and B face and move towards each other. Player A inside-outside dribbles the ball, while player B runs forward without the ball. Player A executes a change in the direction of dribbling using the sole of the foot at the moment he approaches player B. Player B executes a change in direction and, without a ball, runs in the direction of a free marker forming the triangle and traps the pass from player A with an inside touch and then carries out the exercise using the same technique. – diagram 9.

Diagram 9

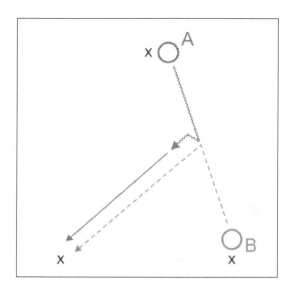

○ The players practice in pairs. Each pair is assigned 8 training markers set out in slalom and one ball. Player A is positioned at the beginning of the slalom with a ball. Player B is positioned without a ball at the end of the slalom. At a given signal, players A and B progress between the markers (player A dribbling the ball with the right and left foot in turn, while player B runs forward between the markers). More or less halfway, the partners take over the ball from each other.

○ The players practice in pairs. Each pair is assigned a playing field measuring 15 x 15 feet indicated by means of 4 training markers. Each player in the pair is in possession of a ball. Player A positions himself with a ball in the center of the playing field and dribbles it in any direction. Player B also places himself with a ball next to one of the markers forming the playing field. Player A turns his back on player B and dribbles the ball using the sole of the right or left foot, all the time keeping his back turned to player B. At the coach's command "ball", player B passes the ball using the inside of the foot to player A, who at a suitable moment must stop his ball and using the inside of his foot pass the ball played by player B back to him and then return to dribbling his own ball. The roles are changed after a dozen or so repetitions – diagram 10.

Diagram 10

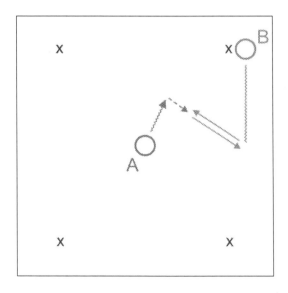

o Players practice in groups of three on half a playing field. Each team is assigned: two training markers arranged three feet apart, a hurdle set at a distance of six feet from the markers and a flag staff set 12 feet from the hurdle. Each player of the three-person team is given a ball. Players from each team carry out the following exercises:

- inside-outside figure eight dribbling of the ball between two markers using the right and left foot;

- then dribbling of the ball and passing it with an inside touch through the center of the hurdle and the execution of a jump with both feet over the hurdle;

- running for a passed ball and execution of a body feint in front of the flag staff;

- return dribbling the ball backwards using the sole of the right and left foot in turn – this exercise to be carried out without any interruption.

Variation:

- dribbling of the ball between markers using the inside of the foot;

- passing the ball using the outside of the foot from the left side of the hurdle and running around it from the right side;

- running for a passed ball with a change in the direction of dribbling by means of a "step over" in front of the flag staff;

- returning by juggling the ball with the right and left foot in turn - this exercise to be carried out without any interruption.

o This exercise is carried out in pairs. Each pair is assigned a playing field measuring of 15 x 15 feet indicated by means of four training markers. Each player of a pair positions himself with a ball opposite his partner and next to a marker, diagonally across the playing field. Players carry out the following motor actions with the ball:

- players A and B, each with a ball, approach each other diagonally across the playing field and at a distance of 2 feet apart change the direction of dribbling the ball using the sole of the foot and dribble the ball to the training marker, from which they began the exercise;

- then A and B play the ball perpendicularly using the inside of the foot (the ball is passed in opposite directions). Player A runs for the ball passed by player B and vice versa. This exercise is then repeated using the same technique, only on opposite sides of the playing field (dribbling of the ball over the second diagonal) – diagram 11.

Diagram 11

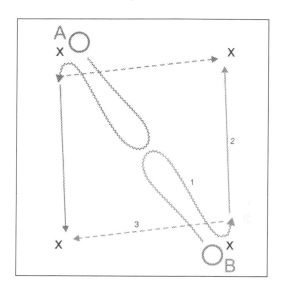

o   The players practice in pairs. Each pair is assigned
    a playing field measuring 15 x 15 feet indicated
    by means of 4 training markers, along with 4 balls
    and two hurdles. We place two hurdles between
    the horizontally arranged markers (one on each
    side). Each player of a pair is in possession of a ball
    and is positioned next to markers on one side of
    the playing field. The next two balls are arranged
    next to free markers forming the second side of
    the playing field. Players carry out the following
    actions:

   •   dribbling of the ball diagonally with take over
       from the partner halfway and then stopping
       it with the sole of the foot next to the marker
       from which the partner began;

- then running forwards without the ball and hopping on one leg over the hurdle;

- then dribbling of the next ball diagonally and the execution of the exercise using the same technique in the opposite direction – diagram 12.

Diagram 12

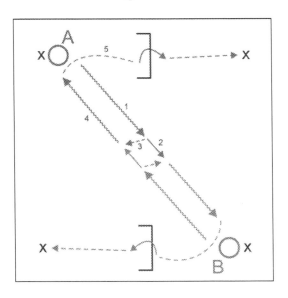

o The players practice in pairs. We use one half of the playing field. Player A carries out a push-up. Player B passes the ball using the inside part of the foot beneath player A's stomach. Player A must then as quickly as possible get up and sprint after the ball passed by player B. The roles are swapped after each pass.

○ The players practice in pairs. Each player dribbles the ball twice with the sole of the right foot and twice with the laces of the left foot and vice versa. Players practice in close proximity. At a given signal, player A stops the ball using the sole of the foot and lies down on his stomach. Player B at the same time passes the ball using the inside or outside of the foot in any direction, jumps over his partner and runs to intercept the ball he passes. The roles are changed after several repetitions.

○ The players are positioned in separate squares with a side of six feet, each with a ball. All squares are marked out with four training markers, arranged opposite each other (6 on each side at a distance of 9 feet apart). Players carry out the following motor exercises with the balls:

- dribbling of the ball diagonally across the square using the right foot in one direction and the left foot in the opposite direction and at a given whistled signal, exchanging the ball using the inside of the foot with the player practicing on the opposite side of the square;

- dribbling of the ball one time with the sole of the right foot and then two touches of the ball using the inside of the foot diagonally across the square and at a given signal, the execution of a straight sit and exchange of the ball using the inside of the foot with the player practicing on the opposite side of the square;

- dribbling of the ball counterclockwise around the square with the simultaneous clockwise dribbling of the ball around a marker using the outside of the foot and vice versa and at a given signal, lying on one's stomach and exchanging the ball using the inside of the foot with the player practicing on the opposite side of the square and trapping using the outside of the foot for dribbling;

- dribbling the ball with a change in direction using the sole of the foot in front of one marker, then in front of the next, a single scissors move with changing direction using the outside of the foot and at a given signal, exchanging the ball using the inside of the foot with the player practicing on the opposite side of the square. The ball may be dribbled horizontally or diagonally – diagram 13.

Diagram 13

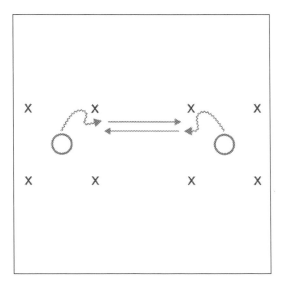

2.3.   The basic learning stage (intended for 10-13 year-olds)

o   The following training exercise takes place on one half of a playing field. Each player is given two balls and exercises in a 5 or 6 foot square indicated by means of 4 markers, plus one flag staff set at a distance of 15 feet from the square. Players carry out the following exercises using two balls:

- dribbling two balls simultaneously within the square, they run forwards to the flag staff, returning by running backwards;

- touching the first ball 4 times using the soles of the feet, dribbling the second ball using the inside and outside of the right foot and dribbling around the flag staff, and on the return, dribbling by the same technique, but using the opposite foot;

- passing the ball towards the flag staff using the inside of the foot and then sprinting after the ball and changing the direction of the dribble, using the inside or outside of the foot in front of the flag staff. The return should be the quickest possible dribbling of the ball back to the square;

- the simultaneous dribbling of 2 balls diagonally across the square, then at a signal jumping up and heading without a ball. Then return to the dribbling of two balls.

o   The following training exercise takes place on one half of a playing field and is carried out in pairs.

Each pair is given two soccer balls. This exercise is organized as above (although the square may be increased to 12 square feet). Players carry out the following motor tasks:

- Players A and B dribble their balls within the square using the sole of the foot and outside of the right and the left foot in turn. At a given signal, they pass the balls towards the flag staff using the inside of the foot and then sprint to intercept the ball just passed by their partner. The return involves dribbling of the ball, using the inside of the right and the left foot in turn.

- Players A and B dribble their balls using (frequent) single scissors. At a given signal, they exchange balls with their partner, using the inside of the foot and then dribble the ball to the flag staff. Returning to the square, the players juggle the ball using just their feet.

- Players A and B dribble their balls using (frequent) single scissors and frequent changes in direction of the ball using the sole and inside of the foot. At a given signal, they jump up and knock shoulders with their partner and then sidestep to the flagstaff without balls. Their return to the square should be backwards, carried out using the same side step.

- Players A and B play one-on-one within the square. At a given signal, the player without the ball leaves the square and moves towards the flag staff. At the same moment, the player with the ball must pass it to his partner, using the inside of the foot, while the partner one-touch passes it back to the first player and they then go back to one-on-one play.

o This training exercise takes place on one half of a playing field. The players practice in pairs. The organization of this exercise is the same as above. Each paired player is given a ball. Player A is positioned next to a flag staff with a ball and dribbles counterclockwise around the flag staff using the outside of the foot. Player B dribbles his ball counterclockwise around the square using the outside of the right foot. At a whistled signal, the players exchange balls, passing with an inside touch and dribbling in the opposite direction, changing the dribbling foot.

o The organization of this exercise is the same as above. Player A stands next to the flag staff and juggles the ball using just his feet. Player B dribbles his ball diagonally, using the sole of the right foot and after a change in direction a front of the marker, he stops his own ball and running without the ball along one side of the square. At a given signal, player A passes his ball to player B, who passes the ball back from the air using the inside of the foot and then goes back to dribbling his own ball, while player A again juggles his own ball. The roles are exchanged after several repetitions – diagram 14.

Diagram 14

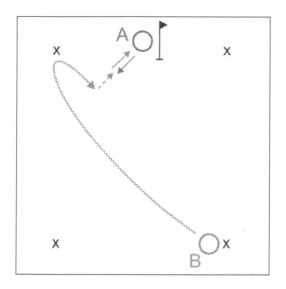

o   The organization of this exercise is the same as above. Player A stands with a ball next to the flag staff. Player B also takes up a position with a ball within the square. There follows an exchange of passes using the inside of the foot and dribbling of the ball: player A dribbling towards the flag staff, while player B dribbles his to the middle of the square. Then A and B change the direction of their dribbling the ball using the sole of the foot (A in front of the flag staff, B in the square) and the exercise begins again from the beginning, using the same technique – diagram 15.

Diagram 15

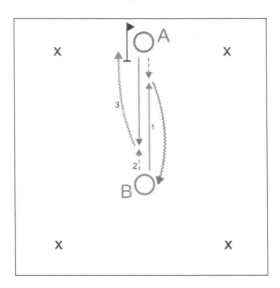

o The players practice in 3-person teams. This exercise takes place in a triangle. Player A is without a ball, while B and C are provided balls. Opposite one of the markers forming the triangle we place four flag staffs forming slalom. The exercise is begun by player B, who passes the ball to player A, then overlaps him and intercepts the return pass, dribbling the ball through the slalom between the flag staffs. After completing the slalom, he exchanges balls with player C using the inside of the foot, and then takes his place. Player C begins the exercises again using the same technique – diagram 16.

Diagram 16

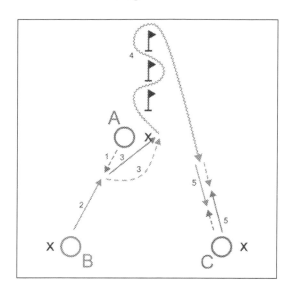

o The organization of this exercise is the same as above. Player A is positioned with a ball next to one of the markers forming the triangle. Players B and C without a ball are positioned one behind the other next to another marker. The exercise is begun by player A passing the ball towards player B, who one-touch passes it back to A, then runs around a free marker and intercepts a pass perpendicularly to the flag staff slalom through which the ball is being dribbled. After dribbling the ball, he passes it to player C, who after trapping it with the inside or outside of the foot for dribbling, passes the ball back to player A and the exercise is repeated from the beginning using the same technique – diagram 17.

Diagram 17

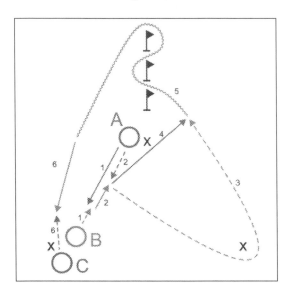

o   The organization of this exercise is the same as above. In this exercise, we use hoops for speed and coordination training. We arrange three training markers in a triangle. Opposite the most forward marker we arrange three hoops, one beside another. The exercise is begun by player A positioned next to the most forward marker. He runs through the hoops, ending with a one-touch exchange of ball with player B and then, intercepting a ball from player C takes his original place, while player C begins the exercise from the beginning without a ball – diagram 18.

Diagram 18

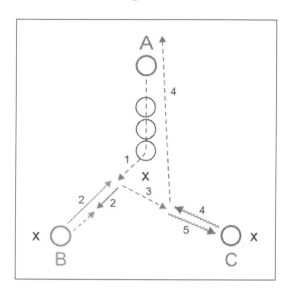

o This training exercise is carried out in teams of three. Each of the teams is given two soccer balls, one hurdle and two markers. The first marker and the hurdle are positioned in a line. The second marker is set at a distance of 20 feet from the first marker. Players A and B are positioned with balls next to the first marker. Player C is positioned in the center between the first and second marker. Player A passes the ball using the inside of the foot to player C, then jumps over the hurdle with both feet and overlaps player C. Then, player C passes the ball again to player A, who changes the direction of his dribbling with the sole of the foot in front of the second marker and returns to the first marker. Player B proceeds using the same technique. The players change places following several repetitions. – diagram 19.

Diagram 19

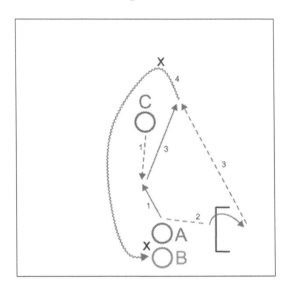

○ This training exercise takes place in teams of three. Each team is provided with two balls and three training markers arranged in the form of a triangle, each 25 feet apart. Players A and B are given balls, while C is without a ball, each being positioned next to one of the markers forming the triangle. Player A dribbles the ball towards player C. Player C executes a slide tackle without contact with the ball or player A. Player A at the moment of player C's slide tackle changes the direction of his dribbling of the ball using the outside of the foot and dribbles the ball to his marker. While dribbling, he stops his ball using the sole of the foot, intercepting a pass from player B and must one-touch pass it back, then return to dribbling his own ball. Player B begins the exercise using the same technique. Players change places after several repetitions – diagram 20.

Diagram 20

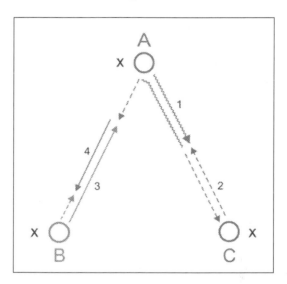

o   On half a playing field we mark out a square 215 feet a side using 4 flag staffs. All players are given balls and practice individually. The players dribble the ball using the inside of the right foot and outside of the left and vice versa without interruption. At the first whistle, they carry out a pass of the ball in one direction using the inside of the foot and start in the opposite direction, while at a second whistle, they sprint to intercept the passed ball.

The time between the first whistle and second should be very short.

o The organization of this exercise is the same as above. The players dribble the ball diagonally using the sole of the foot and with the inside of the right and left foot in turn. At a given whistled signal, they pass the ball with the heel and sprint in the opposite direction. At a second whistle, they sprint for the ball closest to them.

o The organization of this exercise is the same as above. The players dribble the ball twice with the right and twice with the left foot laces and twice with inside touches. At a signal sounded by the coach, the players stop their ball with the sole of the foot and side step to the ball of the closest team mate and carry out a double scissors over the ball, which is lying motionless. At a second whistle, they sprint for their own ball and dribble it using the above-mentioned technique.

o The organization of this exercise is the same as above. Each player is given two balls (size 2 and 4). We arrange a random number of hurdles on the playing field which corresponds to the number of players. Players carry out the following exercises:

• inside-outside dribbling of the smaller ball (size 2) 3 times, using the right and left foot and then passing the ball with an inside touch through the centre of the hurdle, jumping with both feet over the hurdle and then returning to dribbling using the above-mentioned technique;

- transfer to juggling the larger ball (size 4) using just their feet. At a given signal, they kick the ball into the air and trap it from the air with the inside or outside of the foot to dribble it and then pass the ball from the left side of the hurdle, then running around and intercepting it from the right side and transferring to juggling the ball using just the thighs;

- dribbling of the smaller ball using the outside of the foot around one hurdle and with inside touches around the next. At a given signal, they pass the ball in any direction, hop on one leg over the hurdle and sprint for the ball;

- dribbling two balls simultaneously. At a given signal, passing the larger ball in any direction and after passing, the execution of a double scissors over the smaller ball and dribbling it in the direction of the ball passed earlier.

○ We divide half a playing field into 3 equal parts. Players exercise individually, each with a ball. In the first zone, they juggle the ball using just their feet:

- after juggling the ball 5 - 6 times, they execute a turn around their own axis and again juggle the ball using just their feet;

- after juggling the ball 5 - 6 times they trap the ball on their chests and go back again to juggling, using just their feet;

- juggling of the ball using only the right foot as they move forwards, then transferring to juggling of the ball while running also using just the right foot, then at a given whistled signal, they change the foot used for juggling;

- juggling the ball 3-4 times, then kicking the ball up in the air in front of them, sprinting without the ball in the opposite direction and then sprinting for the ball and trapping it from the air to bounce the ball once using the inside or outside of the foot.

- In the second zone:

- Juggling of the ball 5 to 6 times using only the thighs, twice juggling the ball with the feet and then again juggling with the thighs;

- Juggling of the ball twice with the thigh, twice with the foot and at a given signal, trapping the ball for dribbling using the laces of the right foot, with the simultaneous execution of a body feint and then returning to juggling with the thighs;

- Juggling of the ball 5 - 6 times using the thighs, intercepting the ball from the air using the inside of the foot and passing it to the third zone – sprinting for the ball, then trapping it from the air with the inside or outside of the foot for dribbling;

- Transferring to juggling of the ball on the spot 5- 6 times using the head, juggling the ball twice using the thighs and then back to juggling with the head;

o This training exercise is carried out in a 15 foot square indicated by means of training markers. We divide the players into teams of four, who exercise in the assigned areas. The teams carry out the following exercise:

- players A, B, C and D dribble the ball diagonally to the middle of the square, then (being in the center of the square) change direction of the dribble using the sole of the foot and dribble the ball to the starting point, then A exchanges balls with B, while C exchanges his with D (passing the balls the length of the square). After exchanging balls, the exercise is carried out from the beginning using the same technique. All actions are carried out without interruption – diagram 21.

Diagram 21

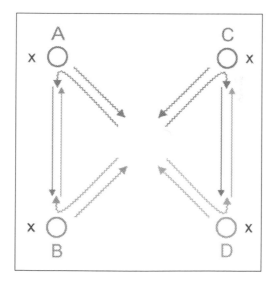

o The organization of this exercise is the same as above. Each of the four team players is provided a ball. Players A with B and C with D pass the balls to each other the length of the square. Then after trapping the ball, they carry out a short dribbling along one side of the square and a single scissors opposite each other halfway down the square: A from B and C from D, then A dribbles the ball to B's position and vice versa, while C dribbles it to D and vice versa. Then the exercise is carried out from the beginning again, using the same technique — diagram 22.

Diagram 22

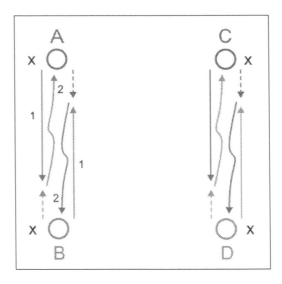

o The organization of this exercise is the same as above. Each player of the 4-person team is in possession of a ball. The players A, B, C and D carry out simultaneous dribbling of the ball around their own marker using the inside or outside of the foot, then change places – A with B and C with D, sprinting without the ball along one side of the square. At the end there follows an exchange of passes with inside touches, along the length of the square: C with A and B with D. Then the exercise is carried out from the beginning again, using the same technique - diagram 23.

Diagram 23

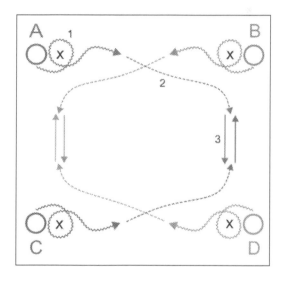

o   The organization of this exercise is the same as above. Each player of the 4-person team is in possession of a ball. Players A, B, C and D begin by lying on their stomachs, getting up each dribbles a ball diagonally across the square using the inside touches. They continue inside-outside dribbling of the ball along the length of the square, exchanging balls with their partners on the opposite side of the square ("take over") and after exchanging balls, dribbling the ball to the position of the partner with whom they exchanged balls. The exercise continues using the same technique – diagram 24.

Diagram 24

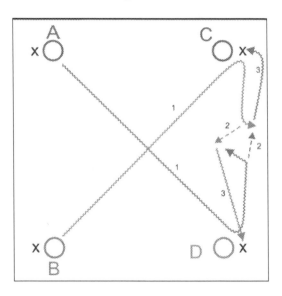

o The organization of this exercise is the same as above. Each 4-person team is provided one ball. Players carry out one-touch passes with an inside touch and then exchange positions with the player to which the ball was passed, for example: player A passes to B, then runs without the ball to player B's position. Player B passes to D etc. After each pass the player passing the ball executes two jumps over a marker with both feet.

○ The organization of this exercise is the same as above. Each 4-person team is provided two balls. Players A and B are positioned diagonally across the square with balls, while C and D without a ball, are also positioned diagonally across the square. Players A and B carry out dribbling of the ball diagonally across the square with a double scissors carried out simultaneously against each other. Then A passes the ball to C, while B passes his ball to D along one side of the square, then players C and D dribble their balls diagonally with a body feint simultaneously carried out against each other and passing the ball the length of the square, C to A, and D to B. Then the exercise begins again from the beginning, using the same technique – diagram 25.

Diagram 25

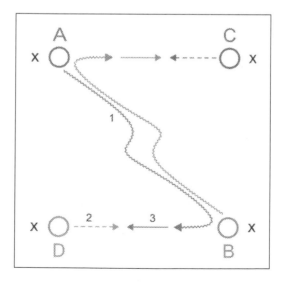

o The organization of this exercise is the same as above. Each 4-person team is provided two balls. Players A and B with the balls in their hands are positioned on one side of the square, while players C and D are positioned without a ball on the other side of the square. Players C and D change places, using the side step as they advance. Once they are at the marker they intercept the ball from the air and one-touch pass it using the inside part of the foot: C intercepting from B and D from A and vice versa – diagram 26

Diagram 26

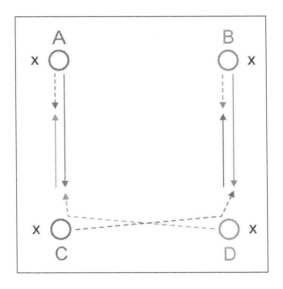

o The organization of this exercise is the same as above. Each 4-person team is provided two balls. Players A and B are positioned with balls on one side of the square and C and D without a ball on the opposite side. Player A dribbles the ball opposite C and B opposite D. As soon as they are near their partners they change the direction of their dribbling of the ball by means of a "step over". After this change in direction, all players return to the starting point and carry out the following tasks: A and B pass the ball to C and D respectively, then overlap them and intercept the pass, B taking the ball back from D, and A from C respectively. Then in front of a marker, A and B change direction of their dribbling the ball and pass it: A to C, B to D. Then players C and D begin the exercise, using the same technique – diagram 27

Diagram 27

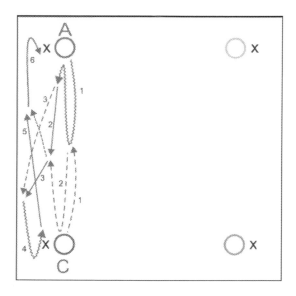

o Players practice in teams of three. In this exercise we use four training markers positioned in slalom and hurdles and three flag staffs. Players A, B and C position themselves next to the flag staffs, while players B and C are not provided balls. The exercise is begun by player A passing the ball to player B and then executing a jump with both feet over a hurdle. Player B one-touch passes back to A, who after trapping the ball, dribbles it through the slalom between the markers and passes it to player C, who also passes the first touch back to A. After the pass, there follows a one-on-one duel ending with a shot at the goal – diagram 28.

Diagram 28

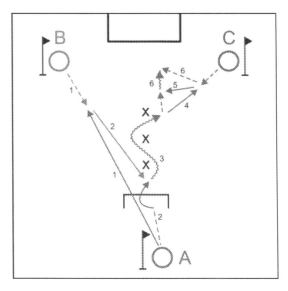

o This training exercise is carried out in twos. Each pair is assigned three markers arranged in a triangle. Player A positions himself next to one of the markers forming the triangle with two soccer balls (one in his hands, the other at his feet). Player B is positioned next to another marker forming the triangle and is given a (size 2 or 1) ball. The exercise takes place in the following way: player B inside-outside dribbles the ball around the marker. Then he executes a summersault and one-touch passes the ball back received from player A, then runs around the third marker forming the triangle and sprints to the second ball (which player A has left unattended) trying to take possession of it in the shortest possible time, and after trapping the ball, dribbles it to the starting point and passes to player A. Then the exercise starts again from the beginning. Players change places after several repetitions.

○ On a whole playing field we create 5 circles with a radius of 15 feet. Each consists of 6 training markers. We divide players into teams of 4. Each team exercises separately in one circle. Teams are provided two balls. Each team of four players is divided into pairs (one ball to a pair) and these compete one-on-one in the center of the circle. At a given whistled signal, players execute the following motor actions:

- sprinting without the ball (all four) and running around any training marker forming the circle and a return to one-on-one play;

- as above, only this time two players sprint with the balls and the other two without a ball, and at the moment they return to the middle of their exercise circle, the players with balls pass them to their partners and then return to one-on-one play

- two players sprint without a ball to any training marker, while the other two dribble the ball in the center of the circle, then pass the balls to their partners who return to the middle of the circles and there follows a return to one-on-one play;

○ The organization of this exercise is the same as above except that players A and B have the balls and are positioned on the outside of the circle next to any marker forming the circle, while C and D are in the center of the circle without a ball. Player C is a defender, while player D is attacking and co-operates with the players standing outside the circle. This exercise depends on player D trying to beat the defender (player C) by balancing his body and changing direction and one-touch passing the ball back passed by one of the players standing outside the circle. He receives a point for each ball passed. The outside players A and B can move with the ball between the markers forming the circle. This exercise lasts one minute, then there follows a change in players.

○ The organization of this exercise is the same as above with the sole difference being that only player A outside the circle is given a ball, while player B is also outside the circle but without a ball. Players C and D play one-on-one in the center of the circle. This exercise involves the player being next to the ball in the center of the field having the task of passing it to the player without a ball and then sprinting to a free position and intercepting a pass from the player outside the circle that is in possession of a ball from the beginning of the exercise. Players receive a point for every successful attempt. The exercise lasts one minute, then the players exchange roles.

○ This training exercise takes place on a 15x15 foot field. Each player is provided with a ball. Players juggle the balls using just their feet. At a given signal, they kick their ball into the air with the laces of the right foot and have the task of intercepting and juggling any ball passed by another player. The players carry out juggling of the ball in the following way:

- using just their feet;
- 4 times with their feet - 4 times with the thigh (smaller size of ball);
- twice with the thigh - twice with the head ;
- foot - chest;
- one time with the foot - one time with the head ;
- Using two balls:
- juggling of the ball using just their feet while passing the smaller ball around the waist clockwise and anticlockwise;
- 3 - 4 times with the foot, kicking the ball into the air, turning on their own axis and renewed juggling with the foot (first the smaller, then the larger ball).

o   Players exercise individually on half a playing field. Each player is given two balls (size 2 and 4) and three markers arranged in the form of a triangle. Each player is positioned in the center of a triangle with the larger ball, while the smaller ball lies next to one of the markers forming the triangle. The players carry out juggling of the ball together with dribbling, as well as dribbling of the ball using the following technique:

- juggling of the ball clockwise around the triangle with just the right foot as they move forwards, then with just the left foot also proceeding forwards;

- juggling of the ball around one of the markers forming the triangle using just their feet and ending by trapping the ball by using the laces and then dribbling the smaller ball into the center of the triangle with a change in direction in front of the markers forming the triangle (changing the direction of the dribble with the sole of the foot);

- juggling the ball using the thighs around one of the markers forming the triangle, ending by trapping the ball using the laces and then dribbling two soccer balls simultaneously around the markers forming the triangle;

- juggling of the smaller ball with the head while running between two of the markers forming the triangle, ending by intercepting the ball on the chest and using the laces, dribbling the larger ball with a single scissors in front of each marker forming the triangle;

- juggling of the larger ball using just the feet, kicking the ball into the air and sprinting without the ball to one of the markers forming the triangle, then returning to the ball trapping it on first bounce. This exercise is to be carried out with the larger and smaller ball in turn.

2.4. The skills perfection stage (14-16 year-olds)

○ The players practice in pairs (one ball to a pair). Each pair also exercises with a stability ball. Players carry out the following exercise: player A executes a balanced sit on the ball, player B stands with a ball in his hands three feet from player A and throws the ball at the head of player A, who heading the ball while all the time executing a balanced sit. After several throws, they change places and the exercise is carried out again, using the same technique.

○ The organization of this exercise is the same as above. This time player A executes a kneeling sit with both feet on the stability ball, while player B throws the ball at the head of player A, who passes it back to player B. The partners change places after several throws of the ball.

○ The organization of this exercise is the same as above. Player B has two (different sized) balls in his hands. Player B throws the different sized balls in turn at the head of player A, who heads the balls back. The roles are changed after several throws.

○ We mark out 10 x 10 foot squares on the playing field (the number of squares depending on the number of players). Players play a small game of three-on-one using two balls of different sizes (for instance sizes 1 and 5). The players' task is to keep the two balls as long as possible. At the moment a defender intercepts a ball, he changes places with the player who lost the ball.

o The organization of this exercise is the same as above, with the difference that we make 3 small open goals three feet wide on a playing field indicated by training markers. Players play two-on-two using balls of various weights and sizes. The task of each team is to keep possession of the ball. A team scores a point the moment it passes a ball through one of the small goals, but the pass must be to a partner from his team.

o The organization of this exercise is the same as above. Players this time practice in pairs, each pair being provided one ball. They play a two-on-two game using two soccer balls. Players score the moment they exchange balls by means of a "take over" or exchange the balls between themselves by passing using the inside of the foot.

o The organization of this exercise is the same as the two-on-two game above. One of the teams possessing the two (soccer and tennis) balls begins the game. The tennis ball is held in the hand by one of the partners of a team. This game involves keeping possession of the soccer ball while simultaneously passing the tennis ball to a partner's hands. Each player on a team who is in possession of the ball has a maximum of three contacts with it.

o The organization of this exercise is the same as above. At two of the four markers indicating the diagonal of a 30 x 30 foot square we set up two hurdles six feet apart. Using markers we also create two small goals three feet wide on both sides of the square. This is a two-on-two game. The players of each of the teams are positioned next to the markers, where the hurdles are set up. At a given signal, players start from each end of the square, jumping with both feet over the first hurdle and simultaneously running around the back of the second hurdle, then run around the markers forming the square and sprint for a ball passed by a constant (the coach or a player who changes places with another person every now and then) who stands to one side of the marked out playing field. The players play two-on-two, trying to score goals – diagram 29.

Diagram 29

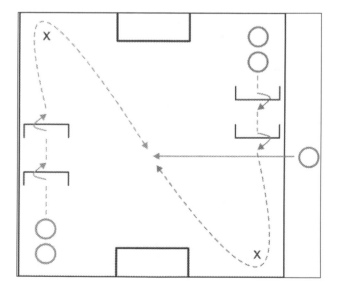

o   We divide a 30 x 30 foot marked out square into four. The game is played in a three-on-one arrangement, where players without a ball must position themselves in the zones closest to that in which a partner with a ball is playing. The maximum number of contacts with the ball for each player is two. At the moment a defender takes possession of the ball, the player who lost the ball changes places with him.

o   We mark out a 30 x 30 foot square, in which players play three-on-one to keep possession of the ball. Each of those playing in the group of three has a maximum of two contacts with the ball. After each pass to a partner, a player must carry out the following exercises:

   a) Jump bringing both knees to the chest
   b) Lie on the stomach
   c) Jump as if to head the ball
   d) Slide tackle.

o   This is a scrimmage five against five. The game is played on a playing field measuring 45 x 30 feet. In the center of the playing field we mark out a square measuring 15 x 15 feet. One player from each team is positioned in the marked out smaller square. A four against four game is played in the remaining part of the marked out playing field. The team scores the moment it passes the ball to a team mate positioned in the smaller square. The task of the player in the smaller square is to one-touch pass the back ball to any other team mate.

o Players practice in pairs. Each pair is assigned two markers positioned 18 feet apart. Each player has a ball. Player A holds one ball in his hands and another between his feet. Player B holds balls the same way. At a given signal, the players pass the hand held ball by heading it, after passing their own to their partner, each must simultaneously inside touches the first ball.

o Here player A has a ball in his hands, while player B has a ball at his feet and each of the players is positioned next to his training marker. Player B passes the ball using the inside of the foot to A, who at the same time throws a ball up in the air. Player A dribbles the ball to B's position after trapping it using the outside of the foot, while B must sprint as quickly as possible and intercept the ball from the air using the inside or outside part of the foot. Then the players change places and carry out the exercise again, using the same technique.

o Players A and B are both provided with balls, whereas player A also holds an additional (size 3) medicine ball in his hands. Players A and B dribble their balls opposite each other and pass: A to the left, B to the right, then they sprint for their partner's ball and dribble it ball back to the starting position. Simultaneously, at the moment of passing the balls, A passes the medicine ball by hand to B. Then this exercise begins again from the beginning, using the same technique.

o Player A is positioned three feet behind player B and is in possession of two balls, one being a (size 3) medicine ball. The players are positioned next to a training marker, with a second marker positioned 30 feet from the first. At a given signal, player A passes the ball along the ground in front of player B, who must quickly react and sprint after the passed ball. After intercepting the ball, Player B changes the direction of his dribbling with the sole of the foot and at this moment A passes him the medicine ball by hand, which B has to catch and then pass the soccer ball he is dribbling using the inside of the foot to A, who after trapping it, dribbles the ball in the direction of B and the exercise begins again, using the same technique, at the marker on the other side.

- Players A and B juggle in pairs, passing the ball to each other 3 - 4 times using the laces. Moreover, one of the players is given a (size 3) medicine ball. As an example, player A juggles the ball, while B holds the medicine ball in his hands. After 3 - 4 times juggle, player A passes the ball using the laces from the air to B, who at the same moment passes the medicine ball by hand to A and juggles the ball passed by A. Then the exercise is carried out again using the same technique.

- On one half of the playing field we mark out several stations of the same shape, namely 4 markers positioned in a broken diagonal each 12 feet apart. At each marker we position two players, the first two players being provided with balls. Moreover at a distance of 15 feet from the markers, either on the left or right of them, we set up 4 hurdles positioned 2 feet apart. The exercise is carried out as follows: Player A passes to player C and runs to his position. Player C passes the first touch to player D and runs to his position. Player D passes the first touch to E and runs to his position. Player E passes the first touch to F and runs to his position. Player F passes the first touch to G and runs to his position. Player G passes the first touch to H, who after dribbling it, passes to B and the exercise begins again using the same technique. After the exercise has been carried out twice, the players jump over hurdles with both feet and return again to exercising with the ball – diagram 30.

Diagram 30

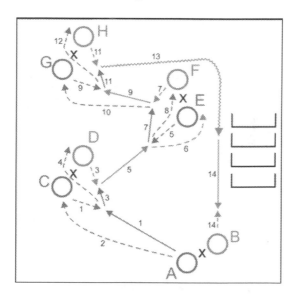

o   On ¾ of a playing field we place two full-size goals and 4 training markers on both sides of the goals at a distance of 9 feet from the touch lines of the playing field. In the center of the playing field, between the goals, we place 4 hurdles positioned vertically on the same line as the goalposts and six feet apart (two on each side). Four players (each with a ball) are positioned next to the training markers. The exercise is begun by 4 players (the first player at each marker). The players carry out the following exercise: from one side and the other, the first player at each marker exchanges passes with an inside touch and after intercepting the pass, they dribble the ball to a hurdle, then they pass the ball through the hurdle and jump over the hurdle with both feet and take a shot at the goal using any technique, then the exercise is begun by the next 4 players – diagram 31.

Diagram 31

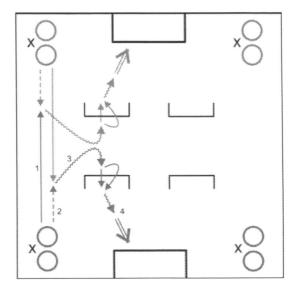

o The organization of this exercise is the same as above. This time, the players hold the ball in their hands. The exercise is begun by   the first of four players at each marker. After a short sprint, they pass the ball from the air to the partner opposite them, using the inside part of the foot, then all four intercept the ball on their chests to their hands, jump with both feet over a hurdle and with the laces take a shot from the air at the goal then the exercise is continued by the next four players.

o The organization of this exercise is the same as above. The exercise is begun by the first of four players from each marker. They dribble the ball with a change in direction halfway, in front of their opposite partner. Then they pass the ball after dribbling it from the right hand side of the hurdle, while running around it from the left and take a shot at the goal, after which the exercise is begun by the next 4 players. – diagram 32.

Diagram 32

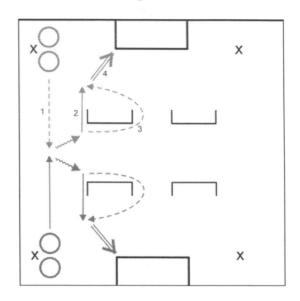

○ The organization of this exercise is the same as above. This exercise is begun by the first of the four players at each marker. The players carry out dribbling of the ball with a pass to the opposite partner at the halfway point. Then they dribble the balls the width of the playing field and carry out a double scissors halfway between the hurdles opposite the next partner, then each of them passes the ball at a hurdle, jumps with both feet over the hurdle and takes a shot at the goal while running full speed.

○ Players practice in threes, each team of three provided with one ball, one speed training ladder and two training markers positioned 3 feet from both ends of the ladder. This exercise is carried out as follows: player A, with the ball in his hands, is positioned next to one of the markers, while B and C are positioned next to the second marker without a ball. At a given signal, B and C run along the speed ladder (C following B) in such a way that they carry out one step left and one step right between each rung and at the end of the ladder heading a ball at a run as it is thrown to them by A. After several repetitions, the player throwing the ball is changed.

○ The organization of this exercise is the same as above This time players B and C work backwards over the gaps in the speed ladder and heading the ball at a run when it is thrown by player A. After several repetitions, the A player is changed.

○ The organization of this exercise is the same as above. This time players B and C move forwards and backwards over the gaps of the speed ladder. Player A holds two balls in his hands. Players B and C, after execution of the exercise, sprint for the balls left behind by A and try to intercept them before they fall to the ground. After intercepting them, they dribble the balls to the beginning and pass them with an inside touch to A. Player A is changed after several repetitions.

○ The organization of this exercise is the same as above. This time we use two ladders, one each for players B and C. Player A, with the ball in his hands, is positioned next to a training marker. At a given signal, players B and C jump on one foot and both feet in turn along the speed ladder and then sprint for the ball thrown by player A and try to win a heading duel in the air. They change places with player A after several repetitions.

o The organization of this exercise is the same as above. We place training markers at the beginning of the ladders, at a distance of six feet. Each player with a ball stands next to a training marker. Players B and C at a given signal dribble the ball, with a pass to their partner, then skip (with the knees brought up high) over the speed ladder, then sprint for the ball passed by player A (the quicker player one-touch back passes to A). The players change places after several repetitions. – diagram 33.

Diagram 33

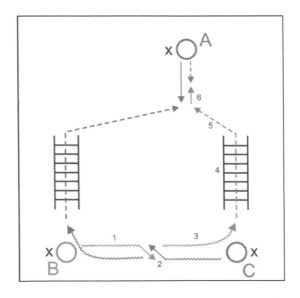

○ We mark out on a playing field several squares (playing fields) with a side of 15 feet. On each of these we place two small goals 3 feet wide and place a flag staff 9 feet from each playing field (this flag staff may be located on any side of the square). Players practice in threes. They are given two balls each. Players carry out the following exercise: player A stands with a ball next to a flag staff, while players B and C play one-on-one in the marked out square. At a given whistled signal, A throws the ball, while B and C sprint to intercept the thrown ball and heading it (this achieved by the player who reacts the quickest), and after passing it they return again to playing one-on-one. After several repetitions, the players change places.

○ The organization of this exercise is the same as above. Players carry out the following exercise: player A is positioned with the ball next to a flag staff. Players B and C play one-on-one in the marked out square. At a given whistled signal, the player who has possession of the ball at that moment (B or C) exchanges balls with the player A next to the flag staff and changes places with him and the one-on-one play recommences.

○ The organization of this exercise is the same as above, except that we set up 4 flag staffs 9 feet from each side of the square. We put a tennis ball on the ground next to the each flag staff. The exercise is carried out as follows: player A is positioned next to one of the 4 flag staffs and holds a tennis ball in his hands. Players C and B play one-on-one. At a given signal, player A throws the tennis ball by hand to the one on one player who has possession of the ball at that moment, and this player, while keeping possession of the soccer ball, must return the tennis ball as quickly as possible and return to the one-on-one play without losing the (soccer) ball. Player A is all the time in motion and throws the tennis ball from the various flag staffs on the sides of the square. After several minutes, the players change places. – diagram 34.

Diagram 34

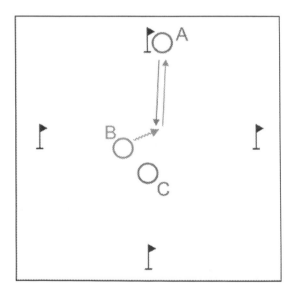

2.5. The training stage (16-18 year-olds)

o Players practice in teams of three. These teams are each provided with two training markers positioned 30 feet apart. Each player has a ball. Players A and B are positioned next to one training marker, while C is next to a second marker on the opposite side. Players juggle the ball with the feet as they move forwards, passing the ball to the partner moving opposite them in such a way that the ball does not fall to the ground. Players juggle the ball using just their feet and are moving forwards the whole time.

o The organization of this exercise is the same as above. The only difference is that players use (size 1) balls. They juggle the ball at a trot, using just their feet and pass it to the next partner. After passing the ball, they lie down on their stomachs and then go back again to juggling the ball.

o Players practice in pairs. Each pair is provided two tennis balls and two soccer balls. Players A and B juggle the soccer ball with their feet and simultaneously pass a tennis ball (each has his own) around the waist. At a given signal, they exchange soccer balls, passing them with an inside touch from the air and juggle them again (balls may not be dropped), simultaneously passing the tennis ball around the waist the whole time.

o Players practice in pairs. Players A and B juggle the ball using just their feet (each has his own ball). At the same time, each player holds a tennis ball in his hands. At a given signal, without it interrupting their juggling, players must exchange tennis balls, passing them by hand.

○ Players practice in pairs. Each pair exercises in a 20 x 20 foot square marked out with four markers, each square having two small goals three feet wide. Players juggle (with one ball) using only their heads (the distance between jugglers should not be more than 2 feet). At a given whistled signal, the players play one-on-one. The player with the ball while they were juggling is designated the forward, while the player without is the defender. After a goal is scored, they return to juggling again.

○ Players practice in pairs. Each pair is provided with a 20 x 20 foot square indicated by means of 4 markers and featuring four small goals 2 feet wide. Players juggle balls using just their thighs. At a given signal, they play one-on-one. The task of the player having possession of the ball at the moment of this signal is to dribble the ball to one of the four goals as quickly as possible, while the player without the ball tries to prevent this. After a goal is scored they return to juggling.

○ The organization of this exercise is the same as above. Each pair is provided with three balls: a soccer ball is laid in the center of the square along with two smaller (size 2) balls, one for each of the players. The players juggle the (size 2) balls with their heads while moving around the square in opposite directions. At a given whistled signal, they must intercept the juggled ball with an inside touch and sprint as quickly as possible to the ball lying in the center of the square and play one-on-one. The player first to reach the ball tries to score and beat his partner. After a goal has been scored the, exercise begins again from the beginning.

- The organization of this exercise is the same as above. Players A and B dribble their balls in opposite directions, each time changing the direction of their dribbling of the ball using the sole of the foot in front of the markers forming the square. At a given signal, the players must carry out a "take over" and stop the partner's ball next to a training marker. Then they sprint for the ball lying in the center of the square and play one-on-one until a goal is scored (the player first to the ball becomes the forward). After a goal is scored, the exercise begins again using the same technique.

- Players practice in pairs. Each player is provided with a ball. Four training markers are positioned in a row three feet apart in front of each player, as well as two larger markers from which the players begin the exercise, and a flag staff positioned in the center, 9 feet from the rows of training markers. Players A and B start at the same time, dribbling the ball through a slalom with inside touches (one touch each with the right then the left foot). After dribbling, player A exchanges balls with player B with an inside touch in front of the flag staff (passing should be diagonal), then both players sprint for the ball passed by their partner, intercept it with an inside touch and change the direction of their dribbling of the ball using the sole, then they sprint with the ball as quickly as possible to the starting point and begin the exercise again using the same technique. – diagram 35.

Diagram 35

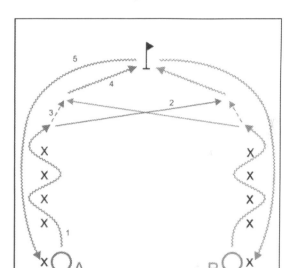

o Players practice in pairs. We arrange 8 training markers on the playing field (in two rows of four). The distance between the markers in the rows should be 6 to 9 feet, while the distance between rows should be 15 feet. A ball is positioned next to each marker of the second and fourth rows. Players carry out the following exercise:

- running forwards to the first row of markers and running backwards between the markers of the first row

- then running side step to the second row

of markers and dribbling the ball using the right foot(both players) and take over the ball by the partner and dribbling with left foot(both partners) after take over the ball

- running forwards with a shoulder to shoulder jump with the partner between the markers of the third row

- running backwards to the fourth row of markers and exchanging balls with one's partner using the inside of the foot after a brief dribbling of the ball between the markers of the fourth row

- then returning using the side step and execution of the exercise from the beginning, using the same technique. – diagram 36

Diagram 36

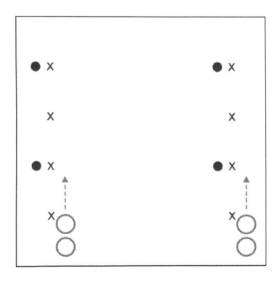

Please note: this exercise should normally be carried out without interruption and at a rapid pace; however, if used during the warm up, it should be carried out at a more measured pace.

o   This training exercise involves 8-man teams. With four training markers we create a square 20 feet a side. Two players are positioned next to each marker. In this exercise we use two balls that are provided to the first players, which are positioned opposite each other diagonally across the square. In addition, we use 4 hurdles positioned on each side of the square. The players with the balls begin the exercise, passing with the inside part of the foot to the next partner and jump over a hurdle with both feet and run to his position. The next players positioned at markers carry out the same variant. Each player intercepts the ball using the outside of the foot to the outside and passes to the next partner using the inside part of the foot.

Please note: after several repetitions, one should change the direction the ball is passed and the direction the players run after passing.

o   The organization of this exercise and the course it takes are as above, with the difference that as often as possible the coach uses a sound signal in the form of a whistle in order to ensure the quickest possible change in direction in the action and the passing of the ball. For more advanced groups, one may introduce three balls.

○ This exercise involves 6-man teams. Each team has a square 18 feet a side indicated by means of 4 markers. The players play 4 against 2 using two balls, the maximum number of contacts with the ball being three. The moment one of the defending players touches a ball he changes places with the player who has just lost the ball. One may limit the number of contacts with the ball to two or even one.

○ This training exercise involves 4-man teams. We arrange four markers on the playing field in the shape of a rhombus. Two players (each with a ball) position themselves next to the markers forming the rhombus and are turned to face each other. The remaining two are in the center (one is a defender, the other a forward). At a given signal, the forward tries with the help of body feints to lose the defender and one-touch play the ball back with one of the players standing next to a marker. The moment the defender wins possession of the ball, the players change roles.

○ The organization of this exercise is the same as above. One of players is positioned without a ball next to a marker forming the rhombus. In the center of the rhombus, the players play 2 against 1. The team with the larger number of players receives a point the moment it tackles the defender and one-touch passes the ball back to the player outside the rhombus. The player who passes the ball must change places with the outer player after passing, and the moment the defender wins the ball, the players exchange roles.

○ The players practice in threes. For this exercise we use five hoops arranged one next to the other and four training markers forming a square 20 feet a side for a one-on-one game. In the center of the square we place three small goals 3 feet wide (we create the goals using markers of a different color). Player A, without a ball, stands in front of the hoops, player B stands on the other side of the hoop with a ball in his hands, while player C is positioned within the square with a ball at his feet. Player A runs through the hoops executing one step in each of them using the right and left foot in turn. After passing over the hoops he passes the ball back using laces from the air to B (player B hand passes the ball to A), then intercepts the ball passed by C with the inside part of the foot as he runs, dribbles it to the square and plays one-on-one against C. Player A wins a point on dribbling the ball through one of the three goals arranged on the playing field. At the moment player C takes possession of the ball, the roles are changed. Player A takes up a position in the square, player C has the ball in his hands, while B carries out the exercise from the beginning using the same technique. – diagram 37

Diagram 37

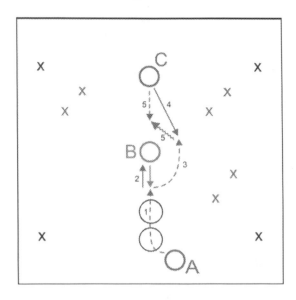

- In this exercise, players practice in pairs. Each pair is provided with two training markers set 15 feet apart. Each player has two balls (a tennis ball is held in the hand and a soccer ball at the feet). Players A and B are each positioned next to their markers and turned to face each other. At a given signal, A and B bounce the tennis ball off the ground and simultaneously dribble the soccer ball to the partner's position as quickly as possible so as to catch the tennis ball before it hits the ground a second time. Then they carry out this action in the opposite direction and using the same technique.

- Players practice in pairs. Each pair is assigned two markers set 18 feet apart. Each player is positioned with a ball next to a marker. Each pair of players is also provided with one tennis ball held in the hand by either of the partners. Players exchange one-touch passes with the inside part of the foot, simultaneously passing the tennis ball by hand.

o The players practice in teams of three. Each team is provided with two training markers set 20 feet apart. Players A and B stand next to one marker, player A with a ball. Player C stands next to the opposite marker with a tennis ball in his hands. At a given signal, player C throws the tennis ball up in the air. At the same time player A passes the ball using the inside of the foot to C and then sprints to his place, trying to catch the tennis ball before it falls to the ground. Player C first touches the ball to B and takes his place. Player B carries out the exercise from the beginning, using the same technique.

o The organization of this exercise is the same as above. Players carry out the following motor task. Player C throws a tennis ball up in the air in front of him. Player A carries out the quickest possible dribbling of the ball assisted by player B, who follows him at a distance of 5 feet. Player A must pass the ball to player C and catch the tennis ball before it falls to the ground. The moment player C intercepts the ball, he executes a single scissors in front of player B and dribbles the ball to player A's position. Player B returns to the starting point and the exercise begins again from the beginning using the same technique. This time the exercise is begun by player A. The player who is playing in defense is changed after several repetitions.

- ○ This training exercise is carried out by teams of four. For each team we mark out a playing field for a two against two game and divide it into two halves (one larger and one smaller). On the smaller half we set up two speed ladders (one for each pair), while on the larger half we position a ball in the center. The exercise proceeds as follows: players run over the speed ladders, jumping and heading the ball between partners, changing places after passing. Both pairs exercise in this way until the whistle is blown. At the whistle, they try to take possession of the ball on the larger half of the playing field as quickly as possible and play two-on-two to keep possession of the ball (the maximum number of contacts with the ball permitted being two). At the whistle, they return to the exercise, changing the way they head the ball (heading the ball at full sprint).

- ○ This training exercise is carried by teams of six. We mark out for each team a playing field for a small game of three against three divided into 3 zones of the same size. In the first zone we set up two small goals 6 feet wide at places chosen at random. If the ball finds itself in the first zone, the team next to the ball tries to keep possession as long as possible and wins a point every time the ball is passed to a teammate through one of the two small goals. The moment the ball is played to the middle zone, players may only touch it twice. The moment the ball is played to the third zone, the players must only pass the ball in the air and try to keep it in the air (with any number of contacts with the ball).

○ The organization of this exercise is the same as above. This time, a team scores a point each time it carries out a "wall pass" in the first zone. In the middle zone however, a team scores each time players carry out a take over, while in the third zone a team scores a point the moment it carries out an "overlap". The team with the highest score in the course of 5 minutes of play wins the game.

○ This training exercise is carried out in teams of four. We mark out small playing fields for each team and play four against four. The playing field must be in the shape of a square divided into equal parts. One player from each team is positioned in each part of the square (one-on-one) and the game is begun by the pair given the ball. The task of the player with the ball is to beat the opponent in his part of the square in a one-on-one duel and pass the ball to his partner from any of the three other zones of the square that has been able shake off a defender and is in a free position that allows him to intercept the ball. A team scores a point the moment the ball finds itself in any of the four zones of the square without it being tackled by the opposing team.

○ This training exercise is carried out by teams of four. We mark out a square 18 x 18 feet using four training markers. On opposite sides of the square we place two hurdles 3 feet apart. Players are positioned next to each marker (two with balls, A and B). The exercise begins with all four players exchanging balls using the inside of the foot: A with B and C with D and after trapping the ball they dribble it and change places. Then A and B jump with both feet over the hurdles and head the ball A to C, and B to D, then return to their places, running backwards. The exercise begins again from the beginning using the same technique, only this time C and D head the ball.

○ The players practice in teams of six. We mark out a square 25 x 25 feet using four training markers. Four players (one at each marker) are provided with balls (two of them holding the ball in their hands). Two other players are positioned in the center without a ball (one a defender, the other a forward). The task of the forward who teams with the outer players is to free himself of the defender (body balancing, changing direction etc.) and head the ball to any of the players are positioned at the markers, who hold it briefly in their hands and then one-touch pass the ball back using the inside of the foot to players who keep the ball along the ground. For every well-aimed pass, a player receives a point. One pair competes for 20 seconds or until the ball is lost by the forward. Pairs are changed every 20 seconds.

○ Players practice in teams of five. Every team is provided with one full-size goal and, at a distance of 30-35 feet from the goal, several training hurdles and markers are arranged at random but close to each other. One of the players is positioned between these hurdles and markers.

The remaining four players (each with a ball) are positioned (A on the left, B on the right side, with C and D in the middle) at a distance of 45-60 feet from the player without a ball. The exercise is begun by player A, standing on the left, who passes the ball in the air to the player standing in front of the goal, whose task it is to intercept the ball and to take a shot at the goal without touching any of the hurdles or markers around him. This player may make contact with the ball a maximum two times. The other players each play a ball using the same technique. The player without a ball is changed after the whole exercise is executed.

o   This training exercise is carried out as above. This time we mark out a 20 x 20 foot square using 4 markers some 30-35 feet in front of the goal. Two players are positioned in the square (one a forward, the other a defender), the remaining three are placed at a distance of 45-60 feet from the players in the square. The exercise is begun by any of the three placed at 45-60 feet passing the ball in the air to the forward, who must free himself from his opponent and carry out a shot at the goal (in this we lay emphasis on the forward having as few contacts with the ball as possible).

o   The players practice in pairs with each pair having one ball. Each pair is assigned two training markers situated 60 feet apart. Players A and B juggle a ball back and forth while in motion. Player A moves forward, while player B moves backwards. The player who is in possession of the ball after four passes juggles it to his partner using the inside of the foot and they both then turn on their own axis, while the partner on intercepting the ball executes the same maneuver (we change the juggling technique, for example: juggling of the ball using only the head).

○ Players practice in fours. Each pair is provided with two training markers and two speed training ladders positioned one on the left, the other on the right. Two players are positioned next to each training marker. Players one-touch pass the ball using the inside of the foot, then run over the high-speed ladder with the knees raised high and again one-touch pass the ball using the inside part of the foot to the next partner.

III. MOTOR COORDINATION AND ONE-ON-ONE PLAY

It is hard to imagine today a team playing in modern soccer and having no players able to play good one-on-one both on defense and offense. It is precisely this element of the game that often determines the final score on the playing field. It is true that soccer is a team game and according to many recognized coaches worldwide, the team should not be dedicated to the benefit of any particular individual. It is hard not to agree with that. However, when we can take good advantage of the excellent one-on-one predispositions of particular players and include this element in a team's style and tactics, then the quality of the team's game will be of a much higher standard. The team will doubtlessly also enjoy a psychological advantage over its opponents. Play against such individuals as: Ronaldinho, Messi, Kaka and many others is particularly difficult, especially when we think of the defenders who come up against the above mentioned soccer stars. An outstanding example in April of 2009 in another sport would be any NBA player that has to defend LeBron James.

The excellence of a particular individual brings rational advantages for the team. It permits the creation of a superiority of numbers in attack and provides alternative execution of a large number of the game's regular elements thanks to the fouls committed against excellent dribblers. It concentrates the attention of the opposing team's defenders on one, two or three players, thanks to which there is more room for the remaining team-mates on the playing field who will find themselves defended against by lesser players. It permits the team to include more tactical combinations in its game due to the excellent practical technique of such players. In the defensive game on the other hand, it allows for good interception of the ball and rapid transfer to counter-attack. According to Milosz Stepinski (2007) "dribbling is a form of play aimed at producing a momentary advantage in numbers in a given sector of the playing field, thanks to which the dribbling player obtains the opportunity to take a shot at goal or execute a pass". The above opinion only confirms how important an element the use of exercises based on the individual game should be in the training of young soccer adepts. I shall go even further and say that a close link exists between a player's individual moments of glory on the playing field and his coordinative motor abilities. One-on-one play requires excellent preparation in terms of speed of reaction, orientation, adaptation, rearrangement and a feeling of rhythm. We must remember to develop the above abilities in one-on-one exercises. The education of both defensive and offensive soccer players for whom the individual one-on-one game represents no threat is only possible thanks to such lessons. To develop this idea further, I would like to note that in principle we see eleven pairs competing against each other on the playing field. Head to head competition takes place in a more or less well-thought-out way in every sector of the playing field and in a very tight space. Taking all of this into account, it is obvious that every modern soccer player must know how to beat his opponent in one-on-one situations both in attack and defense all the time recognizing that soccer players vary considerably in natural talent for the individual game.

Especially today when the players most in demand on the market are universal players, where the traditional roles of defensive or offensive soccer players are disappearing, when the game is played fast and in a diminished space, one-on-one training is of preeminent importance and may not be neglected. If we want to conduct really good training for children, we must have some rational idea concerning their development and have stated goals for their improvement. Individual technique combined with one-on-one play should be developed at every stage of soccer education. The time when the most attention should be paid to this element is the age group between 6 and 12. I say this because modern soccer is based on the speed motor actions are carried out. And we are not talking here about locomotive speed, but about component speeds such as anticipation or perception, which in the main determine the effectiveness and pertinence of the decisions undertaken on the playing field. Young players within the age parameters I mentioned above possess the greatest resources for development of the speed characteristic of soccer. This is the time and place for elements that simultaneously perfect time and speed of reaction and the other components of speed to be introduced into training exercises. In soccer, these exercises must be based on one-on-one play. Similarly, during training we must not forget to apply exercises featuring complex reactions because, as Jan Chmura (2004) reminds us, "proper training is the development of complex reactions", and so we must invent and use exercises in which one-on-one play is combined with all the additional elements arising during a game: passing, shooting, changes in direction etc. Let's remember that exercises must always reflect the actual game and simultaneously develop coordinative motor abilities. We therefore must conduct these on small spaces, constantly changing their formation. In this way we will perfect the ability of orientation. Going further still, let's ensure that during his execution of exercises a player has to deal with various situations that reflect what happens in the game. This will raise the level of his ability to adapt and reposition himself. We need to change the pace of the exercises, which will provide results in the form of a better feeling of rhythm. We will improve the speed of reaction by concentrating on exercises with a considerable coefficient of complex reactions. But we should also remember that simple reactions hardly ever take place during a game. For this reason too, one should not apply (unless in the form of a game) the loose one-on-one play so adored by coaches (without additional tasks or the use of other elements met with in the game). Such a form may be used during warm up or in the form of motor skill games in the initial phase of soccer education. I also would like to touch briefly on one very essential aspect. Namely that during my observations of matches between youngsters, particularly those in the youngest age categories between 6 and 10 years of age, I have more than once heard coaches calling out the instruction: "Don't dribble. Pass!" I can only presume that the only aim such trainers were interested in was the final score of the match. Is this really what working with youngsters is all about? Only winning? Particularly at this most basic stage of learning? Absolutely not, dear reader! It is not the score that is most important, but the effects of this effort in the future. It must be remembered that children in the above mentioned age group will dribble the ball always and everywhere, because this is all their biological and, more importantly, their psychological development permits them at this time. Let them dribble! Let's allow them to enjoy the game because thanks to this enjoyment they learn the often natural and instinctive habits and behaviors of one-on-one play. Let's not hinder in them what at this moment is the most important and enjoyable for them, namely: the ability to sense of where the goal is, to know where the goalkeeper is and, the best part for them, how to defeat "the keep" as quickly as possible. Coaches must maintain a certain distance from what happens on the playing field for players are these early ages. We will obtain the advantage at some future time of a more completely developed and universal player. We shall be able to teach more difficult and complicated elements. The player will master in a natural way, often unwittingly, the simpler elements so necessary to build on in later training years. This will be possible thanks to our giving the young player free rein to dribble and shoot at the goal for it is that which doubtless provides a child at this stage the greatest satisfaction. We must never forget that this should be a goal in itself, on the principle of "results count more than method".

3.1. Example exercises for the improvement of a player's individual game in combination with coordinative elements specific to the game of soccer.

o   This training exercise is carried out in threes. Player A dribbles the ball through a slalom and passes to player B, then overlaps him and on taking a pass from B, takes a shot at the goal. Then he intercepts a pass from the opposite side of the playing field from player C and tries to beat the goalkeeper in a one-on-one situation. The distance between players should amount to a maximum 25 feet. The execution of this exercise additionally requires two goals set 60-75 feet apart, 4 training markers to mark out the slalom and 3 flag staffs indicating the places from which players are to begin the exercise. – diagram 38

Diagram 38

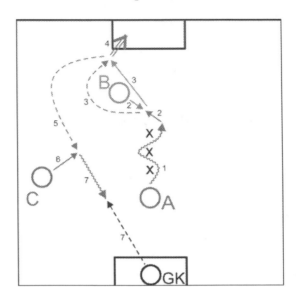

o   This training exercise is carried out in a 30 x 30 foot square, divided into 4 zones. In two of these four zones players compete one-on-one. Neutral players are positioned in the other two zones, their task being to co-operate with the players presently in possession of the ball. A player receives a point for every well-aimed exchange of the ball with a neutral player, but may not pass twice to the same player. Neutral players must change their zones after each exchange of passes.

o   A two against two game takes place on a 45 x 30 foot playing field divided into three zones (the middle zone should be smaller). A one-on-one game is played in the first and third zones. Both teams defend and attack the training markers set out in a row on the touchlines of the playing field. A team scores a point the moment it hits one of these markers with the ball. The exercise is begun by the player with the ball in the first zone, who tries to beat his opponent and enter the neutral (middle) zone and pass to his partner from the third zone. After intercepting the ball, the partner tries to beat his opponent and hit a marker. If an opponent manages to intercept the ball, he must enter the neutral zone and pass the ball to his partner from the first zone, who tries to win a one-on-one duel and hit a marker. After being intercepted, the ball must always be dribbled to the neutral zone in order to pass it to the partner from the opposite zone.

○ We mark out two small goals with a width of 3 feet positioned parallel to each other. The distance between the goals should be 30 feet. Players A and B are positioned opposite each other. They play a one-on-one game and may not cross the parallel line dividing the two goals. The player with the ball scores a point the moment he dribbles the ball to one of the two goals. The player without the ball may only block his opponent at the moment he finds himself level with the goals. – diagram 39

Diagram 39

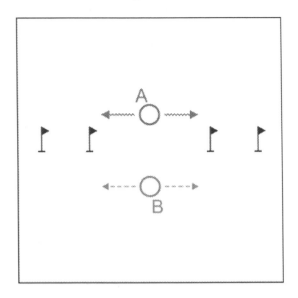

- 4 players exercise in a 30 x 30 foot square, two being provided with balls. All four execute the exercise simultaneously. Players A and B dribble their balls diagonally, while C and D also move diagonally, but without a ball. Then A one-touch exchanges with C and B with D, then A and B try to beat their opponents one-on-one and score a goal. This exercise requires two goals set 60-75 feet apart and 4 flag staffs marking the square and the place from which players begin the exercise. – diagram 40

Diagram 40

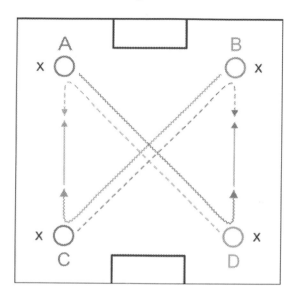

○ This exercise is carried out on a 30 x 30 foot playing field on which 2 foot tall hurdles are placed at random. A one-on-one game is played. The task of that player with possession of the ball is to beat his opponent and dribble the ball through a hurdle. The player receives a point for every well-aimed dribble of the ball.

○ This training exercise is carried out in fours in an extended 30 feet penalty area. Players A and B run through speed hoops (the distance between players should be 3 feet, one playing as a defender, the other as a forward). Then the forward receives a pass from player C positioned on the left or right side of the penalty area. After intercepting the ball, the forward tries to beat the defender in a one-on-

one duel and score a goal. He changes the direction in which he runs after executing these actions and intercepts a pass from player D, who is positioned on the far edge of the extended penalty area. The moment he intercepts the ball, he tries to beat the opponent in a one-on-one situation with his back to the goal and complete the action of scoring a goal. If during this exercise the defender tackles him and takes possession of the ball, he automatically becomes the forward, while the forward becomes the defender. – diagram 41

Diagram 41

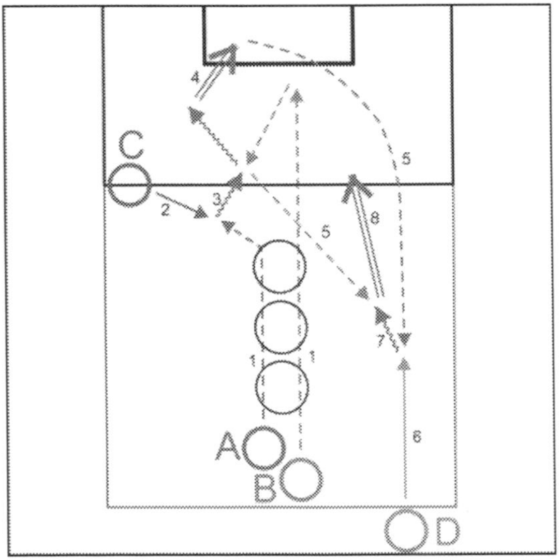

o In this exercise, player A moves backwards and player B forwards with the ball. The distance between the players should not be greater than 2 feet. Player B dribbles the ball using the right and left foot in turn. Player A's task is to keep changing his line and adopt a correct position of the body in relation to the partner dribbling the ball.

○ Players A and B move as a pair parallel to each other. The distance between the players should not exceed 2 feet. Both the partners are provided with a ball. Player A sets the pace and direction of their motion with the ball, using a varied repertoire of dribbling styles. Player B tries to react as quickly as possible and carry out the same actions as player A.

○ This training exercise is carried out by four players in a 45 x 45 foot square divided into two halves of equal size. We place 6 markers on the touchline of one half. Players A and B sprint simultaneously for a ball thrown by C, then jump up and heading the ball (an aerial one-on-one duel). Then they sprint for the second half and a ball thrown by D and play one-on-one until knocking down one of the markers. Player C is positioned opposite the markers. Player D is positioned to the left of the side on which the markers are set up. Players are changed after each repetition of the exercise.

○ This training exercise is carried out on a 30 x 30 foot equal sided triangle. Five players take part: A and B in the center of the triangle, A with a ball. Players C, D and E are positioned next to the markers forming the triangle. A one-on-one game is played in the center. The task of the player with possession of the ball is to pass the ball to one of the players outside the triangle and take his place without loss of the ball. The player scores a point for every successful pass. Each time the ball must be passed to a different player.

o   This training exercise is carried out in a 30 foot long and 15 foot wide corridor divided into three zones. The middle zone is 18 feet long. Players exercise in threes, with one player in each of the zones. The player in the middle zone is the defender. The player in the first zone begins the exercise, his task being to tackle the defender in the middle zone and pass the ball to the player in the third zone. On intercepting the pass, the player from the third zone carries out the same action. One may not pass the ball to the next zone unless one beats the defender in the middle zone in a one-on-one duel. If the defender takes possession of the ball, he immediately passes it to a free player and he himself goes to the zone in which the player who lost the ball was positioned.

o   This training exercise is carried out on a 45 x 30 foot playing field divided into three zones. The middle zone is nine feet long. The game played is two against two + 1. A one-on-one duel is fought in the first and third zones, while a neutral player is positioned in the middle zone and has a maximum one touch with the ball. The game begins in the first zone. The player with the ball must beat his opponent and pass the ball to his partner from the third zone. However, this may only happen after the ball is pass by the neutral player positioned in the middle zone. For every change in zone in the way described above, the team scores 2 points. The team wins one point when the neutral player passes the ball back to a partner in the zone from which he received the ball.

o   We mark out a 10 x 10 foot square by means of four flag staffs on a penalty area extended to 45 feet. Two players + a goalkeeper take part in this exercise. Players A and B dribble balls diagonally across the marked out square and trap them with the sole of the foot next to the opposite flag staffs. Then they sprint for the ball thrown by the goalkeeper in any sector of the marked out field and competing one-on-one, try to beat their partner and score a goal. – diagram 42.

Diagram 42

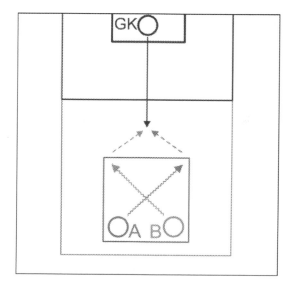

o   We mark out a 45 x 30 foot playing field divided into three zones. The length of the middle zone should be 25 feet and the outer zones 10 feet in length.

In the center of the middle zone we place a 5 foot wide goal, which may be shot at from either side. Four players take part in the game. Players A and B compete one-on-one in the middle zone. Players C and D take up positions in the first and third zones respectively. The task of the player next to the ball is to win a one-on-one duel in the middle zone and try to score a goal. The player receives one point for every successful attempt. The player wins two points the moment he passes the ball to one of the outer players (C or D), in which case player C must one-touch pass the ball to D, and this player in turn passes the ball to the middle player that was in possession of the ball before it was passed to player C. The players change zones after several minutes of the game. Players may not change their zones during the game. – diagram 43.

Diagram 43

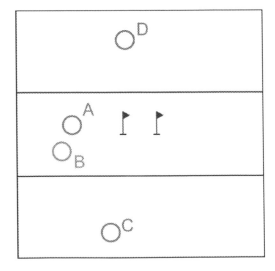

○ This training exercise is carried out on a playing field divided into three zones. The length of the zones is as in the previous exercise. In the middle zone we place three small goals three feet wide. 4 players take part in the exercise. A one-on-one game is played in the middle zone, the remaining two players being positioned in the outer zones and playing with the player who is in possession of the ball. Players may not change zones during the game. The task of the player in possession of the ball is to beat his opponent in a one-on-one game and pass the ball to one of his partners in the outer zones through one of the small goals situated in the middle zone. A player receives a point for every successful attempt.

○ This training exercise is carried out on a playing field measuring 18 x 18 feet with two 3 foot wide goals. The exercise is carried out in twos, each player with a ball. A one-on-one game is played. The task is to take possession of the ball from the opponent while keeping possession of one's own and trying to score a goal. A player can not score goals unless he is in possession of two soccer balls.

IV. SUMMARY

I wrote this book for several reasons. First and foremost is my passion for sport, and especially for soccer. Secondly, because of a strong desire to share my experience and observations on motor coordination and its importance in the training of young soccer adepts and provide practical tips for coaches, instructors and players on how to develop these aspects of the sport. Thirdly, I still find that there is a paucity of publications dedicated to the issue of motor coordination and its importance in soccer, hence my idea and awareness of the need to discuss this question. The game that has thrilled millions worldwide has changed considerably in the last few years. I refer above all to the pace of the game, play without the ball, total soccer, the technical, tactical, physical and mental preparation of players and generally speaking, the shape of player training. The physical preparation is a question of strength, endurance, speed and motor coordination. On the basis of my own experiences and observations, I realized that the skills that this book deals with are either completely neglected in the training of children or else too little time is dedicated to it in the training unit. In view of the above, I have written a book whose essential purpose is to make those working with youngsters aware just how important and inseparable an element of every training program the development of motor coordination should be. The principle aim is to show that without suitable coordinative and technical preparation, young players will be unable to compete at the highest level of this sport's mastery.   Modern soccer is a game based on high speed, requiring from players enormous effort, the making of accurate decisions in split seconds and adapting to many different and often changing playing field situations in tight spaces. Taking the above into consideration, I have proposed a sequence of exercises for each stage of a young person's soccer education. I have tried to ensure the exercises correspond to the conditions of the actual game while at the same time as being strictly focused on coordination, are also simple, sensible and comprehensible for coaches and players. I hope that you have found here a range of useful hints for your everyday work in this field. Obviously the example exercises provided here may and should be changed or modified to best suit the group of players with which you are working. Moreover, this book discusses coordination in both general terms and its components in detail. It shows how and at what stage of training it is best to develop them. It discusses questions concerning one-on-one play and the influence of coordination on this aspect of the game. It shows the common mistakes made and creates alternatives in order to avoid these in the future. If by means of this textbook I succeed in passing on my knowledge to many coaches in various leagues and classes concerning the sensible development of motor coordination in sports training and if this stimulates them to use their own ideas, then I shall consider my purpose has been achieved. I hope this book will be of assistance in the preparation of players for soccer at the highest level.

The author / Pawel Guziejko

BIBLIOGRAPHY

1. Bangsbo, J. 1994. Fitness Training in Football – A Scientific Approach. August Krogh Institute, University of Copenhagen, Denmark.

2. Bednarski, L. 2000. Soccer. Krakow, Poland.

3. Bischops, K; Gerards, H. 1998. Soccer training of children and youngsters, Germany.

4. Boyle, M. 2004. Functional Training for Sports.

5. Chmura, J. 2003. Speed in soccer, Warsaw, Poland.

6. Gambetta, V. 1998. The Complete Guide to Soccer Conditioning. "Footwork for Goalie and Field Play" pages 20-21.

7. Kapera, R; Śledziewski, D. 1997. Soccer. Unification of the process of training children and youngsters, PZPN Warsaw, Poland.

8. Ljach, W; Witkowski, Z. 2004. Exercises for developing coordinative motor abilities in soccer. Central Sports Institute, Warsaw, Poland.

9. Raczek, J. 1989. Youth training in the competitive sports system, AWF (Physical Education Academy) Katowice, Poland.

10. Schreiner, P. 2000. Coordination, Agility and Speed Training for Soccer, Germany.

11. Stępiński, M. 2007. Modern soccer tactics, Poznan, Poland.

AGENDA

○^{A} - Player

○ - speed hoop

● - soccer ball

x - marker

⚑ - flag

⌐¬ -hurdles

▥ -speed ladder

1, 2, 3, 4,.. - fallow numbers

⟶ - pass

- - -▶ - run without the ball

⟿ - dribble

⟹ - shoot on goal

⌢ - jump